King's Cross to Waverley

MADE AND PRINTED IN GREAT BRITAIN
BY
WILLIAM HODGE AND COMPANY, LIMITED
LONDON DINBURGH GLASGOW

BY THE SAME AUTHOR

THE PRIVATE PAPERS OF A BANKRUPT BOOKSELLER.

THE BANKRUPT BOOKSELLER SPEAKS AGAIN.

HADES! THE LADIES!

DOWN BUT NOT OUT.

THE OLD MILL.

KING'S CROSS TO WAVERLEY

A DISCURSIVE DIARY TELLING OF PERSONS AND POLICIES, OPINIONS AND OCCURRENCES IN DAYS OF WAR

BY

TIMOLEON

GLASGOW EDINBURGH LONDON
WILLIAM HODGE & COMPANY, LIMITED
1944.

First Published, - November, 1944

As a diarist I have always liked Dedications. My favourite is the most famous.

TO THE ONLIE BEGETTER OF THESE INSUING SONNETS MR. W. H. ALL HAPPINESSE AND THAT ETERNITIE PROMISED BY OUR EVER-LIVING POET WISHETH THE WELL-WISHING ADVENTURER IN SETTING FORTH.—T. T.

I hope I have remembered and transcribed it aright, because it was in my mind, when I "the well-wishing adventurer" was "setting forth" from King's Cross to Waverley for the first time.

My dedication, therefore, I too must make and it is neither single nor simple.

This book, then, is dedicated to my Minister, to the Secretary of State for Scotland, to the Regional Commissioner for Scotland, to the Lord Provost, Magistrates and Council of the City of Edinburgh, to the Chairman of National Savings, to the Permanent Secretaries and Under Secretaries of all Departments of His Majesty's Government in Scotland, to the Officers Commanding, Ruling or Directing all His Majesty's Forces in Scotland, to these, and to an uncounted score of others, do I make appropriate and full acknowledgment.

TIMOLEON.

November, 1944.

AUTHOR'S APOLOGY

IN a way, diary writing is a weakness. It is self-consciousness, vanity. You feel important—I must really write something—this is a day, I have been alive in it, it cannot just pass to the void as a million million of days have done.

Why do we write diaries, we Pepyses and Evelyns and Barbellions and so forths?

There is nothing really much to tell that any other cannot tell. Our experiences are not unique. I am not one of those who go to Hamburg to bomb it for the first time or travel with Mr. Winston Churchill to see Mr. Stalin. We are all too ordinary and yet—I write as a sedative. It calms me to write in this book with this atrocious pen in this atrocious Commercial Room. It brings me to my resting bed dreamy and content and not wholly feeling that life is nothing.

It is good to be a diarist, if only to check up if need be, the recording angel.

I see myself in a robe with my note books under my arm, appearing on the day of judgment. A pathetic figure, I think, in a way.

I looked at myself in the bathroom at the Cumberland Hotel. Spindlyshanks don't go with a pot-belly, I thought, but the recording angel will overlook that in a diarist.

Diarists are conscientious people. Are we not numbered among those who cry loud hosannas proclaiming, in pencil and in ink, in prose and in verse, legibly and illegibly, in all languages, in all countries, and at all hours—this is the day the Lord hath made and we are His diarists.

AT THE HOTEL IN EDINBURGH Monday

It occurs to me that I am not the first who has done this trip—this road from London to Edinburgh and back again. A simple, childish, vain thought—I recognize it is just that—but it came to me hurtling north last night along the road the Romans marched.

There well may be a traveller's joy—it is a climbing plant—the traveller climbs up hill all the way, even to the very end.

The poets have been kind to us. We who travel hopefully are better than they who stay at home. We get more for our money. I have had enough in to-day's journey—enough, that is, of discomfort, dirt, delay, disgusting company, depression—and anything else that begins with the fourth letter in the alphabet.

The crowning misery was to be invited by a brother civil servant to eat with him. That was too much. I could not abide it. I sought my bed. A Scotsman I might have endured but as Laurence Sterne has observed:

"As an Englishman does not travel to see English men, I retired to my room."

To-morrow I have an appointment at St. Andrew's House. St. Andrew is my patron saint for to-night but I will offer him my solitary prayers.

I may need his help.

Did his Cross not hang in the heavens the night before the battle between Scots and Picts at Athelstane? It is a good omen.

I will play "girded and shod," the hero in the coming day. I am girded and shod for battle.

EDINBURGH Tuesday

THEY are very proud of their Princes Street in Edinburgh but it owes more to nature than to art. A young architect, Robert Hurd, in the Office of Works, emphasized this to me to-day. He thinks it horrible. I heard him being told that the architects like other street and pavement artists might claim it as "all my own work," and this is true. Nature made the rock and the valley, men made the Mound and the gardens, and Lord Provost Drummond drew a straight line along which the houses were built. Hurd would arcade this street of gusty winds and slanting rain like the Rue de Rivoli in Paris, but he hasn't converted any of the shopkeepers yet to his plans!

The fact is the architects have not done too well. The fine buildings of the world don't number more than a hundred, I am told. They are poor seconds to nature. Nature does it every time—the architects only occasionally. Wren, Adams, Haussman, Frederick the Great, Beau Nash, Patrick Geddes—these names directly and indirectly mean good planning, fine buildings, and gracious city life. They were not the only ones at whose doors opportunity knocked. The fact is the architects are better critics than creators. Too many of them think they are Ruskin or Morris rather than men of the drawing board. It won't do. Ruskin and William Morris can be forgotten in their un-read books but what the architects have done, all the world (unhappily) can see for itself.

Let them not be too eager about displaying their works; let them pause and reflect. They are not like those whose names are writ in water. Masonry—mere masonry—alas! is their memorial.

HOTEL, EDINBURGH Tuesday

How wonderful are the W.V.S.! Lady Reading leads the ladies of England but Lady Ruth Balfour controls the clanswomen of Scotland. They are full of good works—stitching and saving and fruit juices and canteen and salvage and all the world that man leaves to his wife. To-day the conference—and the Duchess of Buccleuch and the Lady Rosebery are prominent with many another beside.

Peeresses don't have pride of place unless they pay for it by service and, truth to tell, most of them do in no small measure. Pepys would have loved this occasion and tripped gaily home to tell his wife. It was, as the R.A.F. say, a good party and I had a cup of tea from the Lady Provost of Edinburgh, surely in tallness one of the most eminent figures in the country. She was most gracious withal, though I am quite sure she didn't know my name. I could have told her some things about His Lordship, her husband, but we men must stand together.

The women beat us by their insistence on the monogamic principle. Women believe and practise the strategic theory —divide and conquer. They get us each alone. We are driven to surrender. The odds are overwhelming—too overwhelming.

I overheard a good story. One of the Councillors, an eloquent speaker and very popular at our assemblies, was being rebuked for not attending some meeting. "I have a technique in these matters," he asserted. "I am always being asked and I always accept. This procedure pleases and that is great gain. When the time comes, if I don't feel inclined or have something better to do, I just don't go. I send a good apology—they quite understand how busy I am—they sympathize and I am asked again!" It is an idea. One gains, up to a point, by being willing to oblige apparently, even if one ultimately disappoints.

HOTEL, EDINBURGH Wednesday

WHAT is the place of the building society in the post-war world? I know this much that the building society men are big men whether their names are Bellman or Allison. Bellman is the big man in London and Allison is the ace in Scotland. Conferences don't convey much but walking away from St. Andrew's House to-day I got a picture of the building societies finding the capital, the Ministry of Labour finding the labour, the Ministry of Supply the materials and every Englishman's castle-in-the-air, his home and every Scotsman's mansion in the skies, his cottage.

It is pretty but is it art? as Kipling has inquired. If not art, is it artifice?

Fortunately, the housing of the people is not my department.

There will be difficulties about housing. The politicians are making a mistake in stressing it too strongly. These attacks on the houses we have are sheer wickedness, if there is no prospect for a long time of anything better for most of us.

Let them try another tune—an old tune—one written by an American in Algiers wellnigh a hundred years ago.

There was no H. and C. nor even baths in those days, but its sentiment found a ready echo everywhere. I recall it as I heard it sung in the Albert Hall.

"Mid pleasures and palaces though we may roam,
Be it ever so humble, there's no place like home."

Why do politicians always play up discontent? Should they not seek to enfranchise men of "the all enclosing freehold of content."

EDINBURGH Friday

THIS business of war takes me into unexpected byways. I had not thought to meet, for example, two distinguished civic leaders in one week but so it befalls.

Both of them are concerned about the encroachments of the Government on their cities and they are up in arms. The Lord Mayor of Birmingham and the Lord Provost of Edinburgh convince me that there is more vitality out of London than is generally believed in Whitehall. These two, and I believe they are fair samples, will fight the war without much guidance from those who are just discovering local government for the first time. They were both studying Air Raid Precautions in 1938 and met in Hamburg that summer; two minds with but a single thought.

I prophesy that we are going to have more local autonomy in the future and not less, as some planners indicate.

This regionalization is an old, old story. The Fabians in the nineties knew that, for they called their regional planning scheme in those days the New Heptarchy and even named the English regions, Mercia, Northumbria, and so on. . . .

Parish pump politics I have never despised—what's wrong with a good parish pump anyway? It won't come by nature or by conferences or even as a result of special government committees. Trust the people—at home.

Trust them, I say, with their parish pump.

Let them study it, set it in a fair garden, improve it, redesign it, if you like, until it becomes a fountain both of life and of liberty.

HOME Tuesday

THAT little girl with the plaits, seven sparrows on an apple tree after the rain, the lady from Florence who could not share in the Prime Minister's view of Signor Mussolini, the very scratchy pen stamped "JOHN MITCHELL'S 0261B," the passage in Stevenson's "Pulvis et Umbra," beginning "poor soul here for so little" . . . , these have all been in my mind and under my observation since breakfast this morning and I have garnered them on this page.

Why not? We do waste life. How short are our recollections! It is a pity . . . but we diarists know how precious life in little can be and how we try to imprison, embrace, embalm eternity, the fleeting moment. It is our justification. It is our wisdom. It cuts us off from the gulping, swallowing sort who take life, hors d'œuvres, soup, fish, joint, sweets, cheese, all in one dish and all at once.

We are the miniaturists. We find infinite riches in little room. We have the lovingly microscopic eye. We are travellers in the little things, like W. H. Hudson's acquaintance. Our love is for little systems which have their day. If they have their day, it is enough for the diarist. He leaves to others the decline and fall of empires, the broad sweep of history. His field is a happier one, a more limited one. The sun rises, the sun sets; call it a day.

It is enough for the diarist.

Look on him with affectionate, indulgent eyes—faithfully recollecting—faithfully recording. He is, anyway, not a despairer of life. He thinks it worth while to take pains to have part of it all over again. It is, he flatters himself although you will not, a genius of his, this capacity for taking pains with a diary.

LONDON Saturday

A FUNNY little man, I thought him as I went down home from Waterloo just to see how my house was standing up to it. It was all right. The gardener was funny. He was all worked up about invasion, and his own garden, not mine. He wouldn't stand for it, he said. He went on, "If they trample up my beans and cauliflowers I will be fair mad. I've seen it too—I saw the mess they made of gardens at Poperinghe and Bailleul. Something in me rises against them, those Huns. Why don't they stay at home; what's wrong with cafes in Cologne or hamburgers in Hamburg for Germans? I've seen them too, they're all right. It is very inconvenient for me, it just messes up everything, but I am not going to stand for it. I will not be responsible for myself if they come into my garden and mess up the beans and the cauliflowers. . . . Your garden, too . . ." he said.

"Not only my garden, this suburb, this town, this country—any where they are not invited and not wanted. I would have the Germans know I will resist their invasion. I don't want it and I won't have it. There."

I felt quite awkward with him.

I thought he was going to ask about his dues for looking after my place all these months—but not a word. His heat astonished me, but up north I have been rather out of it. It comforted me as I travelled back to Waterloo.

My garden would be all right.

EDINBURGH, A RAILWAY HOTEL Tuesday

THIS isn't the first diary I have kept. I have always been at it. These hours and days have seemed so precious to me; I who am a pilgrim of eternity like the rest of mankind feel there is something in every hour.

"Quick, thy tablets, Memory!" is the ever present itch of the diarist.

> "Yesterday returneth not—
> Perchance to-morrow cometh not
> Thine is to-day
> Misuse it not."

Diarists feel that acutely. I recommend diary keeping as a prod, a spur, an encouragement; was that what I did with this day ten years ago? I must do better to-day! I am through with my apprenticeship to life; is this all I have learned, is this the best I can make of it—must I be born again—is it for me that the Eternal Recurrence was devised?

I hope not. Please let me be excused. I will do my work better. I will learn my lesson and apply its teaching. Let these be my petitions and my prayer. "If thou dost love life," said worldly-wise Yankee, Benjamin Franklin, "then do not squander time, for that is the stuff life is made of."

Let me be energetic, go to the ant, thou sluggard, get your work done, death stands at your elbow, be thou about thy Father's business . . . for if not, when you come to-morrow to this diary you will have nothing to record, nothing attempted, nothing done to earn even Samuel Pepys's benediction, "and so to bed."

OFFICE, LONDON Wednesday

"No taxation without representation," used to be a slogan when I was a young Liberal. It was a good principle—he who pays the piper—as the Scotch say—calls the tune.

It is incredible—some think—that any would pay for a piper but there is no accounting for tastes—especially musical taste.

But is one entitled to vote because one pays taxes?

If one is, there is a lot of liberty being denied, a lot of rights refused.

I have paid for a bottle of whisky. There is a lot of taxation and not much whisky in that price. If the theory is to be upheld the whisky buyers are entitled to a great deal more of a say in the government of the day, and I don't want much insight to see what they would say on their ballot papers.

And why not?

Universal suffrage is no sounder a basis whereon to erect a governmental system than buying whisky or tobacco. Counting any heads is just as absurd as counting lively heads or smoked ones.

Was it Mr. Dooley who wrote "Drink never made any man better but it makes him think he is better."

Local veto should be for the individual, not the locality.

A case would be made for the boozers—the nicotine addicts—the cinema gazers with their entertainment tax—they have their vices—but how much of the burden of the virtuous do they carry—and for how much of it do they pay in pursuit of their pleasures!

EARLY HOME Saturday

SHAKESPEARE has come to his own again. He has had his ups and downs, but the B.B.C. is right in finding in him the authentic voice of England—England at war—England fighting for her very existence.

But the English have not always been so kind to him.

So simple and orthodox am I that I have always enjoyed Shakespeare. He wasn't a school task for me. I found him naturally and comparatively late in life. Frank Harris's "The Man Shakespeare" was one of the roads by which I reached him and Logan Pearsall Smith and Dover Wilson, too, have pointed me the way.

But there have been others. I have some notes in one of my Shakespeare books that make me laugh outright. Mr. Wells, in an article in the Strand Magazine, opines "What did Shakespeare do, what did he add to the world's totality? . . . He had none of the power and patriotic pride of Milton. If he had never lived, things would be very much as they are. . . . He added no idea, he altered no idea, in the growing understanding of mankind."

And Mr. Shaw, "With the single exception of Homer, there is no eminent writer, not even Sir Walter Scott, whom I can despise as entirely as I despise Shakespeare when I measure my mind against his. . . . To read 'Cymbeline' and to think of Goethe, of Wagner, of Ibsen, is for me to imperil the habit of studied moderation of statement which years of public responsibility as a journalist have made almost second nature to me."

How tolerant the English are of humbugs. It is a national vice.

No wonder the Germans think us poltroons!

HOME Sunday

No one who writes a diary is free from curiosity about other diarists. Gibbon is my favourite. I like the man. His "Journal," it has been said, has not the verve of Byron's Diaries, or the artless candour of Pepys's, but it has all the marks of keen observation, of indomitable industry, and omnivorous reading.

He had something to write about, too; born at Putney, school at Westminster, Oxford and Lausanne, it would make almost any dolt a man worth meeting and fit to keep a journal.

His declared object, he wrote on 24th August, 1761, was "to keep an exact journal of my actions and studies both to assist my memory and to accustom me to set a due value upon my time."

A journal can have a wider field. Arnold Bennett made his a source book.

For the life of me I don't know why I write one, but it is a habit now incurably formed. I do sometimes neglect my daily page but I always sleep badly on these nights when I have had a bad day; a few minutes writing my page puts it into proper perspective. What annoyed me is not worth writing down, and therefore not worth worrying about and so, purged by offering entries to the diary which are refused for their unimportance, my mind eases itself and I come to my resting bed, weary and content and sure of slumber. The cares that infest the day do not disturb my sweet repose when I have done my diary.

LONDON Monday

DOWN home for a week, away from breezy, wheezy (it gets my chest) Edinburgh, my housekeeper has been at me for waste paper for the Salvage Campaign. She does not know that I flee Edinburgh to escape these busybodies, busy on any busyness but their own, she does not know and I do not tell her.

She is a good housekeeper and in spite of great temptations to eat another's rations, she keeps my house and still remains—my housekeeper!

I fall for salvage. I rake and I rummage. I seek and I search. But I throw out little. I find it difficult to part with papers, with letters, and certainly parting with books is no sweet sorrow, it is pain. But I suffered to allow some books to pass from me, a Co-operative Annual, the Daily Mail Year Book of 1936 (I could well have kept it, it once was up-to-date, it is now history, or at any rate an historic document), some pamphlets and two coverless Newnes's sixpennies of years long gone.

A poor contribution, my housekeeper thought, but then she is in the W.V.S. and that affects any woman's judgment, I hasten to add, not adversely. I kept one book although twice had it in mind to throw it away. It is a school book. My name is on it in round, unformed, school-boy writing. The date is 1899. The book is "Lyra Heroica," a book of verse for boys.

It will have to go next salvage drive, I am convinced, so I transcribe some words from Henley's Preface. He never wrote better. He tells of the object of the book: "To set forth, as only art can, the beauty and the joy of living, the beauty and the blessedness of death, the glory of battle and adventure, the nobility of devotion—to a cause, an ideal, a passion even—the dignity of resistance, the sacred quality of patriotism—that is my ambition here."

That will do for to-day, I think aloud as I close the pages of this diary.

HOTEL, EDINBURGH Tuesday

My life, this year, seems strung between the two capitals—London and Edinburgh. I leap to the smooth, inevitable cliché, my life is a Tale of Two Cities!

In some ways it is for me the best of Dickens. "The Tale of Two Cities," of course, is more Harrison Ainsworth than Dickens, which shows I am not a real dyed-in-the-wool lover of Charles Dickens. I like him—not at his best but at his worst.

There are not a few writers who have similar allegiances. There are as many lovers of Sir Walter Scott's "Talisman" as there are admirers of his "Heart of Midlothian"—and Stevenson with "Treasure Island" commands a larger following than ever he won for his "Lay Morals" or for his "Edinburgh—Picturesque Notes."

I am back in Edinburgh again and I confess I like the place the better every time I come to it. The scoffers tell me it is the food. It is true enough that even in these days one fares better at the de Guise or L'Aperitif or the Peacock Inn than one does anywhere else in this Island.

Certainly London isn't in it; but then the Londoners are stoic practisers of austerity. They are model citizens. They have won these days—without Dickens—the world's applause.

No longer is it London for food or for entertainment or, indeed, for life. It is "London for Heroes"—and the world knows it!

Outside of London we are commoner clay; commoner, but more comfortable.

HOTEL (MINISTERIAL LUNCHEON) Wednesday

"PRUNES—yes—prunes—I genuinely like them." The lady at lunch with me was genuinely surprised and, I think, astonished. "Prunes," she said, I think indelicately, "I only take them for medicine." Shades of California Syrup for Soothing Softness!

She was a demure piece and had had education. I suspect her lover was killed in the 1914-1918 war—not that she knew it—O! no. Is it realized that there are in the British Empire over one million women who might have had husbands if one million men of the British Empire hadn't been killed in that war?

I don't mean these women were engaged. They simply hadn't had time to meet their boys.

But prunes, I genuinely prefer them. They are essential

to the war. Prunes—for one Cabinet Minister, two Members of Parliament, and several officials of the Ministry of Aircraft Production—are PRIORITY NUMBER ONE.

Lord Woolton has—charming word—released them. They are available at all the six places at which I have eaten this week.

They are chosen; it is true they are the only choice, but what of it? There is a destiny in these things although we cannot discern it. Did Dickens, I wonder, ever imagine they would be controlled when he wrote of "Papas, Potatoes, Poultry, Prunes and Prisms"?

EDINBURGH Thursday

THEY do it well in the City of Edinburgh! War or no war, the Lord Provost and Magistrates of this Ancient City which has shown me so much hospitality still maintain the traditional ways.

To-day I was one of the company. The Lord Provost and his council wore red robes trimmed with ermine and they were escorted and guarded by halberdiers and sword-bearers.

I had the curiosity to inquire what these gentlemen did in days of war other than carrying the sword and the halberd and the pike. They are soldiers and sailors of other wars, I saw by their medals, and for the rest, have duties under the corporation as custodians of the City Chambers as they call them.

It is well that tradition—appropriately dressed—lives among us. It began in Edinburgh with its first Lord Provost William de Dederyk in the 13th century. He must have been, I conjecture, some wandering Flemish Knight who won himself to the high place of this city. His name and the names of all his successors are painted on the wall in the entrance hall of the City Chambers, and a brave list they make. Soldiers, Politicians, Peers, Lords, Baronets, Knights, Tradesmen, Merchants—and some mere gentlemen—they and I and my official portfolio are joined to a living past. Edinburgh lives, not because she is alive to-day, but because she has roots.

Roots is an appropriate word. Sir Robert Greig, one time head of the Scottish Agricultural Department, opens the National Campaign for Allotments—not allotments of cash for soldiers' wives as one member of the audience thought—but allotments of land whereon to grow potatoes. The Secretary of State said the war will be won maybe by him who has his hands on the last potato.

I hope it won't be too hot a one!

HOME FROM THE WARDENS' POST — Saturday

THE historian, I hope, will not in his survey of these times fail to observe the growth and initiative of voluntary societies in war time. The Local Defence Volunteers rose unbidden by authority and their subsequent official shape as Home Guard will not obscure their spontaneous and more honourable origin; more honourable in that they owed nothing to the "direction" of the Ministry of Labour.

And there are many others.

The early Wardens, those who before Munich days, strove to fit themselves for the wrath which they felt in their bones was to come to their country; the week-end fliers for whom time held in its womb the Battle of Britain as their destiny—these must not be forgotten men and women if history is written aright. . . . But neither they nor I, it is borne in on me, will read that history if it is written.

"A hundred years from now, dear heart,
We will not know—nor care
What came of all life's bitterness
Or followed love's despair."

Who wrote that? I cannot remember.

Life comes to that—a few lines of poetry—recollection and regret. All these tense months and weary years lumped and heaped and humped together add up to that; that and a very strong cup of tea in the Wardens' Post to-night which tea is now, I faintly conjecture, causing me indigestion.

AT HOME Sunday

There are compensations. The ledgers are balanced. We get our deserts.

This has been a bad day for me—a difficult day. I will not recount the difficulties. Sorrow's crown of sorrow may lie in remembering happier things. I seize gladly the crown of sorrows. There are happier things. I will embrace them.

So I compose myself. So I put the day behind me.

My eye lights on something. I left these papers in my "in" tray and there they lie. I have been looking at them. I have laid down my pen. What are they?

Rate demand and income tax demand lie neatly in a file

with accounts for the family, accounts from the grocer, a premium notice from the insurance company. They lie neatly in a file. The file is in the left-hand tray of the desk with the words UNPAID ACCOUNTS written thereon.

(That girl was very neat at lettering . . . it is a pity about her and that fellow—was it the Tank Corps?)

The file is in the left-hand tray and I stare at it blankly.

It is very comfortable here.

The glasses and the bottles are on the oval tray. The whisky is suddenly arresting.

I am not arrested, however.

I am free.

I go on.

Thanks, I *will* have another.

This will balance my ledger for to-day.

This is my desert.

LONDON OFFICE — Monday

THE agnostic is no longer with us. I have not met one for years and yet in my early days they were as common as cobs in Kent.

It was a fine attitude—for attitude it was. We have been a fearful race of mystified savages, worshipping sticks and stones and rituals and mysteries too long to be over certain that we did not know. We know, all right. We know fear and hope—we cannot resist the conviction, against all evidence, that human life is a bit—a little bit maybe—of all right. We are not easily weaned from the god our ancestors found in the mighty rushing wind or in the rumble of the earthquake.

We know all right. The B.B.C. have been at us with a Bishop and some other Ministers—not to mention my friend the Lord Provost of Edinburgh—telling us "Why I Believe in God."

It wasn't a very satisfactory series. We do not domesticate the immensity even if the medium is the ether.

We still take the wings of the morning and He is there with the Royal Air Force. The Sub-mariners know He is in the depths of the sea. There are no agnostics among brave men. They would indeed be braver men than they are—and the breed does not disappear from among us, High Heaven be praised—they would indeed be braver men if they entered battle with the strange thought in their minds that they did not know that the Lord Reigneth and that all the seas and the air and land are His.

Arnold Bennett said the finest thing in the Bible is "Be still and know that I am God." The agnostics are still these days—very still.

EDINBURGH Tuesday

WE are a poor people. We will be poorer. We all had great possessions—foreign investments—all, all are gone, the old familiar places in our national budget.

We are a poor people. The tale has been told to me of two Edinburgh men. They were sent to the United States and Canada to realize our investments. I say "our" investments. They weren't mine. They, probably, weren't yours. They were the investments of English and Scotch who, seeking a profit, financed many enterprises over the Atlantic. That was in days gone by. The first Great War left them more or less still British Investments. In the intervening years, we even added to them by our inventive, our trading and our manufacturing skill.

And then came 1940!

There was no option. We had to realize all U.S.A. and Canadian securities. Two Edinburgh men did this work. They were named Carlyle Gifford and Innes Stewart. It was months ago. I never heard of it. The Treasury knew. The Bank of England knew. Few others knew.

I reflect on the modesty, the noble anonymity of many who serve, and serve conspicuously, their country.

The work over the seas came to an end. There was nothing more to sell, and quietly these two returned to their offices.

As far as I know no one said anything about it. I saw one of them in Charlotte Square to-day—next the house in which Douglas Haig was born.

HOTEL, EDINBURGH Wednesday

THESE are dark and sanguinary hours. The pages of history, once a solace by comparison, no longer reveal any grander picture than the one which all around presents itself.

The Dark Ages seem about to descend, all the darker because man has seen something of the light.

Yet, so amazing a creature is man, that it can be recorded that an hour ago an Australian soldier with an Irish name asserted to a casual passer-by in the streets of this Capital City of Scotland, in response to an inquiry how things went with him, "Not too bad, mister, not too bad."

It is not unworthy of that other Observer who, it is recorded in the Book of Genesis in the Bible of the Protestant Christians, "saw everything that He had made and, behold, it was very good."

This habit of under-statement is a national virtue and it has proved an acceptable export. It has done us a lot of good—more good than harm, I am convinced.

Bombast, boasting, braggadocio, they don't go with the climate of our minds. We know we stand alone. We know we have been and are something in the world. We have fought and can fight. We work well together.

We really are a community—a nation.

We are without doubt the greatest people in the world but if asked to appraise our own achievement, the rank and file of us would not admit more than what we have done in the world is "not too bad."

EDINBURGH OFFICE Thursday

THE organizers of war savings—my Lords Kindersley and Alness—do they know what they do? Here in Edinburgh, where I write this fine morning, I learn that one hundred million pounds has been invested in War Loans in Edinburgh through National Savings Appeals. Edinburgh has about half a million inhabitants. That is two hundred pounds each—men, women, children, and visitors. This is stupendous and, as I verily believe, it is not wholly exceptional; what does it augur for the post-war period? This vast purchasing power; is it not a volume of blank cheques on the future, cheques which can only have value—goods and services—if we ourselves provide them?

These hundred millions are the earnest of our determination to produce, to work, to earn.

Nothing encourages a man to work more than the desire to clear off a debt, a bank manager once told me. I hope he is right.

Savings impress me more than planning. Planners are going to spend what the savers have saved. I don't trust them. Let the savers do the planning and the spending which the planning entails. It will be better so. The tailor cuts his own cloth with more care when he has paid for it.

I would put Kindersley and Alness on the Central Planning Committee when it is set up. There is something said about he that pays the piper calls the tune. I am all for that. Savers should be assured now that their savings will not be cast fruitlessly, frantically or futilely away.

ARRIVED AT KING'S CROSS — Saturday

IT will not come. It is the lobster. I shouldn't have taken the brandy. These were my thoughts last night as I rumbled along in the sleeper provided for me by the Ministry of War Transport from Waverley to King's Cross. I couldn't sleep. I reflected upon trains—trains which are so much a part of my days—and, alas!—nights.

Sleep did come at last. It was not the counting of sheep that brought it. I have discovered another and better way. Even if you have eaten the lobster and absorbed the brandy and the coffee—it—my plan—works. You disrobe —undress—slowly. You do your teeth. You arrange yourself. You put out the light. "I'm not going to sleep," something announces in your brain. You fear IT is right;

you are not going to sleep. Then you begin. It is no use counting sheep or reciting the Books of the Bible—even The Lord's Prayer fails. You are in a train. Train—for better or for worse it is. All right, train it will be. I am in a train—how many carriages—how many sleeping berths—first and third—the engine—the driver and the fireman—the guard (who stays at Wembley)—the conductor whose boy is in Sicily and is going in for law at Cambridge—you review them all—they are all in the train. But there are other trains—the Flying Scotsman—the Chicago Flyer—General Sir Bernard Montgomery's train—refreshment cars on the Great Western—how good their toasted tea cakes used to be—the slow train, Appin-Ballachulish—and the tiny one that goes from Kandy to Newera Eliya in Ceylon—there are trains and trains . . . and there are training animals (is it cruelty?)—and train bands and training for the 100 yds. and train-bearers and a train of thought. . . . I fell asleep—train bound.

HOME | Sunday

WE are a lucky people—or are we God's chosen? If the Colonel is to be believed, we are God's chosen. I said flippantly "God's second choice, surely!" and, honest, sincere man that he is he shamed me by ready agreement.

He is a British Israelite and does not agree with that shortest of English poems

"How odd
Of God
To choose
The Jews."

He thinks it rational that the righteous should be chosen and even more rational that we English should be the Second Choice.

It suits me—I put it no higher—to believe that we are right and righteous and that the God of Righteousness has chosen us for His purposes. The world with all its load of injustice and misery, wrong and suffering, spins true on its axis. We think it is good, and means good. There is a divinity—a divinity, mark you, that shapes its, and our, ends. Great men and good men have lived by that faith.

"One lesson," says James Anthony Froude, "and only one, history may be said to repeat with distinctness and that is that the world is built somehow on moral foundations and that in the long run, it is well with the good and ill with the wicked."

O! Lord, help thou my unbelief. Some of the things I have seen these days almost shake my faith.

EDINBURGH Monday

THIS talk of post-war planning is just talk. The talkers will win. It is too easy an art—the making of public speeches.

What have you done? That is the question.

Robert Greenwood Tarran is a man. Chief Warden of Hull these five years, a joiner by trade, he has an idea. He knows the need, the hunger, for houses and he can supply them by his new devices and materials. They are not houses like Hampton Court. I imagine they are only beautiful in the sense that wherever a home is there is beauty. I have no doubt they, and those like them, will have few friends among those who live in lovely Kew Green or gaze entranced from the windows of Moray Place over the Firth of Forth. But men who have tramped the desert or trailed in the retreating columns of Dunkirk and Narvik will not be so critical.

Let us have two housing programmes now and later, let us build useful houses quickly on properly made foundations and laid out in a good plan.

That to begin with.

Then when we have more labour, clearer ideas, better material, remove these First Plan Houses and build better ones on the same foundations. Let us not build for all time. Time is fleeting. Let us have houses now and build increasingly better on these sites.

Let us have rebuilding plans as well as new construction. Every city should review its housing annually; there should be continuous reconditioning, remodelling. Let us start at all houses 100 years old or more—then 90 years the next year, and so on—until no house, internally at any rate, is more than 20 years old.

That will do for my life time.

OFFICE, EDINBURGH — Wednesday

THERE are very good letter writers to-day. I am convinced that they are as good as those which we are taught to believe are classics. I often preen myself that this diary is as good as Pepys's, but no one would believe me.

The Duke of Wellington walking in the park was stopped by a stranger, who, hat in hand, said, "Mr. Smith, I believe." "Sir," said the Duke, "if you can believe that you will believe anything," and strode on. I return to the letter writers. Here is Jimmy Jackson's letter. He was with me at Wadham and retired, or should have retired, before the war. He writes me now once a month and this is what I get to-night. He likes being a warden.

"What a pity," I thought as I slung my respirator and tin hat over my shoulder, "I did not go to Vancouver. I had the money and Cousin Joe wanted me to come. After all, I am over 60. . . . I had earned my retirement as things go. Yet, when I got to the wardens' post I really wouldn't have missed it. Ella Home's brown eyes, the post cat with the short tail, Captain Percy James Halibut, Retd. I.M.S., the Divisional Controller with his curry-ruined digestion, the picture loaned by Mrs. Sherwood, alleged to be by Greuze—none of these would I have seen and known by heart if I had gone to Vancouver. This is the better part, I said, and thank you I will have a cup of tea—no biscuit, no sugar, please."

I think that's good writing. It is a picture at which, if they have eyes and imagination, they will stare in 2043 A.D.

EDINBURGH TO CLYDEBANK — Thursday

BEFORE the war my idea of happiness was a long journey on the Highland Railway—any part—in a first-class carriage—alone. It was more than happiness: it was my peculiar paradise, a paradise of comfortable navy blue coloured upholstery tricked out with little lace mats on which to recline an entirely satisfied head.

Before the war—the glory is departed—that Elysium is in the eternity of the past which returneth not.

To-day I have had two journeys; Edinburgh to Glasgow —Glasgow to Clydebank—and the carriages—they depressed, disillusioned, disgusted me—they make me despair.

Edinburgh to Glasgow was bad, perhaps worse than I saw, because the carriage was full, but it had visible two panels of back upholstery cut and torn. Glasgow to Clydebank had all the electric globes broken at their sockets: the seats were ripped and ragged. The windows—two of them—out altogether, the window straps were gone, the racks stringless.

Slightly disfigured, the notices about "careless talk" glared at me. They had been obeyed—implicitly. There had been no careless talk in this carriage. There had been no idle hands, if idle tongues had been silent. I see the calm, relentless determination to destroy, to destroy purposelessly but finally, utterly. It is significant. They were makers of the engines of destruction, those who had preceded me as passengers from Glasgow to Clydebank. They were the forerunners. They were the pioneers. They were breakers down of privilege.

They were breakers-up of a civilization which was dear to me, the comfort of a first-class carriage.

EDINBURGH, HOTEL Friday

THERE is far greater knowledge in the Civil Service than is publicly supposed. They are very knowledgeable people, civil servants, and their side lines are even more valuable than their official business.

Jackson, for example, regales me all the way from Edinburgh to Perth on Rabelais.

He began just as we got through the huddle of corporation houses which lie west of the City of Edinburgh and I think that he had still much to tell me about Rabelais when we parted at the cloakroom in Perth station. I had to confess that Rabelais, to me, was the man who had given the qualifying adjective to Rabelaisian stories. Rabelaisian stories were the kind of stories which were too dull for the public bar and not quite suitable for the drawing-room. That is, I think, a fair estimate of what most of us know of Rabelais, but Jackson told me about "Gargantua and Pantagruel." Apparently Rabelais did not like the times he lived in. The Reformation was not exactly his choice of the best of all possible worlds but he concealed and embroidered, overlaid and camouflaged his philosophy. Jackson declares that his method was allegorical in that he presents himself as a clown and a glutton, a somewhat contemptible, comic figure, and through these obscurities he tells his philosophy. Those who knew him personally declared that he would be an enigma to posterity because his contemporaries saw in him merely a buffoon, one who could speak very freely and finely when he had had a good dinner when, as a matter of fact, that was not his real character. He knew the folly of human affairs. He could laugh at the vulgar and the great, he was profoundly conscious of the ridiculous which brings low all the high posturing of man . . . he was a satirist . . . he was an ironist . . . so it went on. I took up the *Glasgow Herald,* turned to the financial page, but Jackson went on. Nobody had ever listened to him so intelligently, it appeared to me. I folded up the *Glasgow Herald* and relaxed for the rest of the railway journey. . . .

I think Rabelais would have laughed. . . . I think he would have seen in Jackson and me no less ridiculous figures than those with whom he lived and mixed so many centuries ago.

Of all the talk of Rabelais, now that I am home again (ah! home—this yellow patterned wall paper in this battered caravanserai)—this only do I recall and I record. When Rabelais died, his will and testament declared: "I owe much: I have nothing: The rest I leave to the poor. . . ." Rabelais would like to think that I was impressed with his wit on the way by rail from Edinburgh to Perth.

I am sure he would.

I am sure he is.

LONDON OFFICE Monday

CROWDED railway carriages are, on long journeys, the real House of Commons in this war. The Members of Parliament rarely use them, if I am to believe the fortunate few who claim first-class sleeping compartments from the North to London.

I am more fortunate than the fortunate few, because I get public opinion, albeit somewhat compressed and concise.

Plans for the future, in one carriage from York to London, were of a personal character. The Atlantic Charter seemed a somewhat watery business as indeed one would expect. It seemed as valuable to my fellow passengers and as familiar as the Declaration of Independence or the terms of Magna Charta.

They were all in the services. One intends to be a priest.

One wants to go back to take over the hotel-garage that his father and mother run at Llandudno, "I was going to be a teacher," said a young sergeant pilot, "but that's O.P.H. now. I'm going to Canada when this is over. My best pals are Canadians," he averred. None cared for the dream of a classless society. None cared for the socialization of the means and instruments of production. None adhered to any political party.

It gave me a lesson. It made me glad in a way I was only a temporary bureaucrat.

I will not be one of those they hang on the lamp posts, I will have escaped again into civil life, my labours of these days for the State forgotten. Although neither priest nor hotel-garage keeper nor yet backwoodsman, I will remember that—under discipline, fighting for democracy—their dream, as mine, was to be free to do in life as they wanted!

EDINBURGH Tuesday

It is bad enough to face life alone. I am fortunate in an obscure parentage, but how must it feel to be a Cecil or a Churchill, or even a Rosebery?

The conference was important and Lord Rosebery handled it with really consummate skill. Naturally, most of us approached it under his chairmanship with memories of Liberal Imperialism, "The Last Phase," and large linen collars with marked peaks on them—in a word we thought of Lord Rosebery, one time Prime Minister, and for too short a time a figure in our troubled life.

His son, Harry, as his intimates call him, is a different figure, but not inferior. He is a man of the world without being a worldly man. He is shrewd, comprehending, understanding, and all without any affectation or pose. In fact, poise is his suit. It is all the more creditable for he hasn't my advantage. I am "out of the everywhere" as George Macdonald has it, "into here." He comes, he, and his like, "trailing clouds of glory."

It is a handicap. It is all the more admirable when it is surmounted with, apparently, effortless ease.

I doubt if he likes his task, however, we civil defenders are not the society to which he was born or the society to which he turns naturally. Yes, he was considerate. He was very considerate to one rather obstreperous person. I wonder why. On reflection, I think I know; he had a horse-like face. Rosebery has his sympathies.

Rosebery understands dumb animals. He knows how to train them—even to win races. . . .

> "Blind to Galileo on his turret,
> Dumb to Homer, dumb to Keats. . . ."

EDINBURGH Thursday

THEY gave the Freedom of the City to the Prime Minister to-day but I was not among the invited. Why should I be? I am not a citizen of Edinburgh, I am often reminded, I am a mere passenger. I am neither a Londoner nor a man of Edinburgh, I am one that oscillates between King's Cross and Waverley.

I saw him, none the less. I was fortunate. He seemed well. He arrived at the Waverley station and I saw him as he drove in a car with the Lord Provost into Princes Street. The two seemed to talk familiarly, there was none of that aloofness which most of us feel in the company of the great. I have seen it. The Mayor sitting bolt-erect beside some distinguished Royal Person or an eminent Statesman and those who beheld wondering how they came together and how happy they both would feel when their joint appearance was over! The Scotch are not very demonstrative. They don't even wave handkerchiefs as Londoners do. (Somebody told me that very few Scotch carry handkerchiefs.) Women feebly wave their hands and men, with decorum, lift their hats—not with a gallant sweep but merely four or five inches above the cranium to let the wind blow between their hair and the hatbrim.

The cars turned west along Princes Street, sped away towards the Usher Hall where the ceremony was to take place. I wanted to hear it on the wireless to-night but I got back too late. It is a pity because I like to hear the Prime Minister and I would have liked an invitation. But when I saw the hordes in the hotel, American reporters galore and even a Spaniard, I knew I could get first-hand information! From them I learned all about it . . . what Harry Lauder sang, how the Lord Provost made a speech, how the orchestra played "See the Conquering Hero Comes," . . . the "old man," as they called the Prime Minister, was in great form, stamping his feet and waving his arms and responding generally to the uplifting enthusiasm of heaven knows how many thousands of Edinburgh citizens, who at little cost to themselves, have conferred on him the Freedom of their ancient city.

He left mysteriously, I think, by train. At any rate, all I know is he came, he saw, and he conquered the citizens. Thank heaven we have such a conqueror. Thank heaven we have someone who can take this highly individualistic community and make them think and act and feel like one.

OFFICE, EDINBURGH Friday

SINCE I took up this appointment with the Ministry I have seen three Secretaries of State: John Colville, Ernest Brown, and Thomas Johnston. They have no common characteristic that I can discover.

Colville was a sober Scot, I thought, patient, understanding—a reliable minister. Ernest Brown was only on the job for a little while, but he was, for an Englishman, surprisingly acceptable. His experience of the Scotchmen in his Constituency of Leith must have taught him much. Johnston is of a different mettle. The propagandist idealist applies his ideas to his task. It is not easy. He has his discouragements but he has united Scottish public opinion most successfully. I hope his influence will last. I think it will. He impresses me as a man who has got everything he wants for himself. He isn't after anything except Scotland, and for its welfare, betterment, progress he would give all.

Gone, apparently, is the ardent propagandist of a political theory. He has no theories now—he asks is this desirable, practical, worth while, and if so—on with it. Don't inquire—don't stop—don't write about it—don't harangue—don't ask if it is Christian or Marxian—on with it. This turbulent intensity commends itself to me. He knows he has his chance, his opportunity, his hour, and he wants to give it all to Scotland. And then? They ask, but I have not heard his answer. I prophesy he will one day go to Fintry and write his book. It will be worth reading and he will enjoy writing it.

LONDON Sunday

"Trust thyself," said Emerson in his essay on Self Reliance, "every chord of my being vibrates to that iron string."

Self-confidence is worth cultivating. It yields a worth-while crop.

Trust thyself, but trusting others is a different business.

To expose oneself is dangerous and the risk of septic wounds is real. A wise man keeps in most things his own counsel or at best confides them to his diary.

The time and the place and the loved one altogether is a temptation to confidence which should be resisted. You never know. It is as well to keep one's armour on, never to be wholly unburdened.

There are few—I have found none—who can bear complete candour. Their eyes narrow, they watch you curiously, "fancy him thinking and saying that," they reflect, and an easy friendship is gone for ever because one went too far.

"Aye keep something tae yersel', ye wouldna' tell tae ony," is the quintessence of wisdom, or, if you like it in even homelier phrase, "never give yourself away."

I reproach myself. I am too open. I am too candid. I want to be honest with my friend and I only succeed in exposing my weaknesses to him and so forfeit his regard.

I admitted. I confessed.

I said "quite frankly," and, sin of commission, I meant it.

I was frank—too frank, and I fear I have forfeited a friendship.

The Psalms have it:

"I take heed to my ways that I sin not with my tongue. I will keep my mouth with a bridle."

AT HOME, BEFORE LEAVING FOR KING'S CROSS Monday

SEVERAL things help. Early tea, a friendly "good morning," a greeting about the weather—they all help to begin the new day which the Lord hath made. Some pray, right down on the knees beside the bed, some do stretching exercises, a few read devotional books—Thomas à Kempis or "A Serious Call to a Devout and Holy Life"—I have done them all and there is a time for each of them.

The best thing, and I know all about the fruit salt business and the cold bath, the best thing is the morning paper.

I am deeply moved every day with this miracle of modern life which comes to me to teach me to play the hero in the coming day. It does that. The morning paper tells you how humanity faced it yesterday—how it went on and faltered not—how those who fell—fell in accordance with the tradition—facing the last enemy. Whether it is a *Star* or a *Scotsman* or a mere *Mail* or *Express* or a *Herald* of one sort or another, it is my morning paper that makes me willing to go on with it.

The press hasn't failed—papers—printers' ink—printers, publishers, pressmen—they have not laid down their arms and neither will I!

Life had meaning yesterday, will have meaning to-day, will have some thing to relate to-morrow.

Hail, the morning paper: it is for me, a town dweller, more than all the morning stars that dance together in the dawn on the rim of the world.

EDINBURGH Tuesday

ALL these diaries I have kept—has it been worth while—where are they now?

It has been worth while. Of that I have no doubt—"no possible, probable shadow of doubt—no possible doubt, whatever," as Gilbert wrote.

Diaries are a sort of stocktaking of the day—a residue—a dividend—a remainder and a reminder—a reservation of the dead hours, or, I become poetical with a pen in my hand, a vase into which you place the loveliest, the most interesting flowers of a summer's day.

I don't regret any of my diaries and I have most of them still in the desk at home or in the upper drawer which tops the boot cupboard. (One of the many disadvantages of this travelling life is boots. I do like a different pair of boots every day. Seven days—seven pairs of boots—it is a sybaritic ideal, but so satisfying. They don't write about boots much—these authors—Kipling's "Boots . . . over Africa"—H. G. Wells's "Misery of Boots"—but how little attention do authors pay to fundamentals!)

Some are just pocket diaries. Several have the delightful name of LETTS—what a gorgeous name for a diary manufacturer—LETTS—what hope! What a challenge! not just safety first—or what happens—but an eager LETTS—and so I fill up the little spaces which he lets me have for each day.

The journal diary is the best—about two or three hundred words a day. That is good—I have found it so—not too long—not too short—the Happy Medium for a DIARY.

EDINBURGH HOTEL Wednesday

ONE should cultivate occasions—birthdays, anniversaries, winning the Derby, a son and heir is born, prize for the largest cabbage or the biggest potato—these are occasions and the wise man makes the most of them.

To-night's occasion, however, was 25 years and three weary wanderers from the south like myself, two from Supply and one from the Board of Trade, dined in the Royal British Hotel. (They call it "The Royal British"—how broad minded the Scotch are. It never occurred to them to call it "The Royal Scottish." They go back to the Pict-ish origins for their nomenclature.)

The Royal British Hotel in Princes Street has never been able to find me a bed although I have often offered it the opportunity to accommodate my tired and weary body on its hard, soft or coppersprung mattresses. They are always too busy. I think it is the hotel where the cognoscenti congregate but we booked a table and took our place in the dining-room for our celebration.

Food—it was well enough. One of the celebrators told me that Sir James Peck, the Chief Food Controller for Scotland, invariably goes to the Royal British for his luncheon, but he wasn't there that evening and possibly that justified our having even a better meal than is usual. But it wasn't the meal nor the company—it was the champagne . . . rarer these days than ever and more beautiful than ever. I enjoyed the champagne. I made the most of it and I certainly took the most of it though Board of Trade was an authority. He knew them all. He had been to the champagne country. He had stayed in the Coq d'or in Rheims. He had even met the redoubtable Ribbentrop who, before he was a leader in the Third Reich, at any rate counted himself at least a Count in the champagne world. I was quite glad to have the lecture but don't remember very much about it because I had some old brandy to follow.

Champagne, let me note in this diary so that I may use it as a work of reference when it ceases to be a daily consolation, was first made 250 years ago by the Benedictine Monks. The name of the inventor was Dom Perignon who discovered the art of making the wine sparkle. He had great difficulty over the corking. "In fact, there would be no champagne to-day," said Board of Trade, "if corks had not been developed, because prior to that linen rags and other textile substitutes were used for keeping wines in bottles."

Meditatively I crossed the road, glancing up at the Castle on my right, hoping there would be another anniversary, hoping some day there would be more champagne and more, and more . . . but it was, I recognized, a hope that might not be realized.

EDINBURGH Friday

WALKING up Charing Cross Road last night in the dusk on my way to King's Cross, I lingered by the book shops.

They are not what they were when I was young, but Bertram Dobell with his memories of James Thomson and his "City of Dreadful Night" link me to my struggling days when I was hungry for everything from food to fame. In one of them—the names are different now—opposite Dobell's, I saw a little Edinburgh print. It was Walcot's view of the University and I remembered I had never just seen it as he saw it. This afternoon, escaped from the Cross of St. Andrew in St. Andrew's House, I walked south past the *Scotsman* office, over the Bridges, as these Edinburgh folk call it. It was with a little difficulty I got myself into the exact place from which Walcot had made his picture. You must go almost to the Surgeons' Hall and then you get the height of the dome, the pillared portico and, slender, down the slope you have the spire of the Tolbooth. It was an exquisite evening. "The smoke ascends in a rosy and golden haze," as William Ernest Henley had it when he looked on this old gray city.

I turned into the quadrangle of the Old University and walked round. The lovely lads, now dead and rotten, of 1914 to 1919 have their memorial. Their names are there and fine phrasing tells how they "turned without fear or question from these Gates of Learning to those of the Grave in order that free men might still continue to learn freedom."

The unrelenting struggle goes on in this generation, I mused. The price is never final, it has to be paid again and again. A man—probably a lecturer—maybe a professor—noticed my interest. He seemed grateful for it. He most likely served in that war. He told me as we walked toward the tramline that this was a different war. I concurred. It was a planned war. There was not the volunteering spirit; it existed but it was exceptional. I didn't know. Seven thousand Edinburgh Graduates served; over 900 died for their country; five won the Victoria Cross, he asserted. I lifted my hat and wished him good-day. It was not possible to tell him how I felt. It would have been ridiculous to tell him that I was there because of a little picture by Walcot which I had seen in a bookshop in Charing Cross Road the night before—quite ridiculous, and yet so is life bound together by the apparently trivial and the accidental. Yet I wish I could have told him. He might have understood and been less saddened by the thought of those who, as Edinburgh's Stevenson had it, went down to "the gates of death itself loyal and loving to one another."

Of course, I had forgotten, R.L.S. was at that University. Perhaps it was Stevenson who spoke to me; Stevenson revisiting Edinburgh where surely his heart always lay.

Perhaps.

HOME Saturday

VOTES of thanks always make me feel slightly sick, especially when the proposer is a woman. If the proposer is a man I hope, sometimes without substance, that he has been asked at the last moment and is speaking sincerely, albeit falteringly.

But a woman!

I know she was told three weeks ago. I know she has prepared the speech, rewritten it several times, rehearsed it several times, faced her husband's bored and acid criticism; I know she has gone through all these phases and yet, with the determination of Bloody Mary, or more correctly, Queen Mary First, I, and the audience must hear it out to the last syllable of recorded words. I am sorry for the proposer of the vote of thanks but I am sunk in mind—in slime—in scum when I get up to reply.

My nightmare always begins "Ladies and Gentlemen, it gives me the greatest pleasure. . . ."

And yet that is unfair!

We men are unjust to women. We have kept them in bondage all the days of their lives and we expect them to be both subserviently respectful to us and, when occasion arises, our equals. We ought to make up our minds.

Are they inferior creatures? If so, they should be kept in their place, publicly and privately. If not, we should give them their place with both hands, and the place they want—anything they want. It is only in full possession they will arrive at renunciation.

Let us be just to them—apparently—when we agree to destroy them by offering equal pay for equal work.

AT A HOTEL IN EDINBURGH Monday

SOME men are born to conquer, some are born to be loved, some are born to lead, but are they fortunate whose names in advance suggest these qualities and attributes?

Names, I suppose, matter a good deal. Could, for example, a National Leader come into being whose name is Hinchingbrooke and is not a man unfortunate endowed with such a name as Ramsbottom? Are we safer with our F. E. Smiths and Ernest Browns? Is a common name best for the leader of the common man?

Two men lunched with me to-day, drawn together by the fact that they served in the last war, and, apart from these common experiences which they had enjoyed or endured they fall into the category that names shape destiny.

One of them is Duke—R. N. Duke, C.B., D.S.O., M.C. —distinguished Civil Servant—and the other is Darling. (I don't know whether he has the C.B., but he has many letters after his name, the Lord Provost of Edinburgh.) But while a Duke may lead, is a Darling necessarily endeared? Are these names of theirs an advantage in their careers or a disadvantage? Do they discount their achievements or attainments or do they present them with a handicap? Duke—I never hesitate to write in this book what I think of my colleagues—has more merits than most for the kind of tasks to which he is committed. Scotch, of course, in origin, he was at either Oxford or Cambridge when the last war broke out—as a youth saw bitter fighting—in circumstances of great gallantry won the Military Cross—was a fighting soldier all through the war and must have found it irksome in the lower reaches of Dover House, toiling over Bills, Administration, and other Scottish problems.

He has risen far since these days. I have seen him as a shaper and guider of Civil Defence in Scotland and he is now a rising star in the Air Ministry or some other equally heavenly heights.

Duke is his name; his name seems to have carried with it no handicap—for his leadership, I think, is accepted.

"Darling" means "a little dear." I refrain from elaborating whether this name is a handicap to him or an advantage.

Does it really matter?

EDINBURGH Tuesday

DINNER parties in war time are not the least manifestation of national courage. I sit down replete; the dinner party finished at eleven, I think a very proper hour. My hostess, a careful accumulator of food and wine for many years, a real cupboard-lover, had drawn generously on her stores and her imagination. The menu is worth setting down.

I may not be asked again and anyway I am not likely even at that house ever to dine so well as long as the war lasts.

We guests, eight of us, assembled in the library and there was sherry, South African, I suspect, but decanted; gin and British vermouth and a bottle of Dubonnet.

Upstairs we went for dinner to a pleasant dining-room with a round, bow shaped wall—an Adams inspired house, I fancy. For hors d'oeuvres, there was smoked salmon and a bit of lemon—flown from North Africa we were told and bought at a Red Cross Sale for £2. Clear soup followed and claret or whisky was offered. I drank the claret copiously and had a bit of chicken with mushrooms and beans and small round roast potatoes. The sweet was a triumph, a tinned triumph, of course—peaches and cream—the cream, it was confessed, being whipped condensed milk worked up for an occasion. My savoury was named Guiche Lorraine, King George V's favourite, cheese and strips of bacon; I had two helpings!

The women had Kummel, the last in the country, but I had brandy . . . and walking home felt I had taken farewell of a better world than this generation can ever hope to see.

It was not a facile "au revoir" alas, I fear it is, indeed, "Goodbye."

EDINBURGH, AFTER A HOUSING CONFERENCE Wednesday

WASHING clothes is one of the preoccupations of this city of—I think the Americans call it—"my assignment."

It is surprising how many things I am discovering. Wash-houses are one of many public services. I have seen them in London, I vaguely remember—one surely in Lambeth—but here there are several of them. The wives in Edinburgh, they tell me, used to wash their clothes on the western side of this hotel, in the depression which is now, apparently, filled rather mockingly by the railway which runs through the Princes Street Gardens, so the washing of dirty linen in public is not seen nowadays.

The City Fathers and Mothers—for I am told there are a great many women members of the Edinburgh Town Council, which justifies my writing "Fathers and Mothers" —have provided these wash-houses in most of the densely populated areas. These densely populated areas are places where most of the tenements are situated. In Scotland tenements are blocks of flats of ten or twelve houses grouped round what they call the "common stair." These buildings—two or three rooms each mostly—date in the main from the days before interior sanitation was established, but have water, gas and electric light now. There still is a good deal of limitation in the facilities for washing. Sinks for dishes and the like are general but no tubs, and it is to these tubs that the Scotswoman's mind turns with traditional interest. The town council have erected elaborate wash-houses and to them the housewife goes with her basket of clothes. For a few pence she gets hot water, the use of tub, wringer, drying machine and iron. She can do her own and probably one or two of her neighbours' washing in one forenoon and be back home in time for her man's dinner.

This arrangement strikes me as a contribution to the problem of finding adequate housing for the people who will live closely packed in cities. We do not wash clothes every day—once a week is often enough, and so, as part of the planning, there will be an increase, I am inclined to think, in wash-houses, highly specialized, well organized, adequately supplied with hot water, which can be used for an hour or so every week. Houses are valuable in so far as their parts are continuously used. It is a waste of space and capital invested to have a washing-room in every house when such a place is only used so very occasionally.

These observations come to my mind because of an ardent young captain who sat at my table at lunch. He has charge of a portable washing machine unit in the army, an interesting, composite vehicle which takes dirty clothing in at one end and delivers, after the cleaning and drying process, at the other. He is a laundry expert in peace time, in a very big way, and has an idea that even permanent wash-houses such as Edinburgh has, may give way to the travelling laundry which will plant itself in the street, collect the soiled clothes from 7 till 8, wash, dry, and press the garments and return them to the housewife without having taken them far from her eyes during the whole process. It is going to be a world, apparently, on wheels as far as laundries in the future are concerned, according to my young friend who learned with interest about Edinburgh's wash-houses, but said he had no leisure to examine them, so busy was he with the soldiers' clothes just now. Washing dirty linen in public, then, would seem to be our fate, and who will mind it so long as it is washed really in public and is really clean as a result of the process?

OFFICE, EDINBURGH Wednesday

THIS duty—I object to the phrase "job of work" which

most of my colleagues in the department use—takes me often to Scotland.

Frankly, I like it.

Indeed I like the Scotch. How absurd these humbugs who insist on "Scots" or "Scottish." I like the Scotch. I dislike the Scots, whom the Picts, if they had done their job, would have exterminated, and as for the Scottish, they remind me of the skittish Scotch women teachers on a fortnight's holiday at Ballachulish.

I like the Scotch.

Scotch whisky, Scotch tweeds—what more do the Nationalists want?

I am content with Scotland and the Scotch.

They are—they don't mind French words, I find, naif. One Scotchman told me in the lift going up to my room in the North British Station Hotel in Princes Street, Edinburgh, that the Scotch were the finest people in the world. He didn't know me, he had only a few minutes to impart the information, but he could not resist the duty of telling me of his country's greatness.

It is wonderful. We mustn't be deterred by it. They not only believe in themselves but they have grounds for doing so. We must learn to like them.

Much though we English make of the Scotch, we must do more. I would avow, not because of my lecture in the lift, that Scotland is the most important part of the British Estate. I am a convert—a Scotophile. We must not neglect our assets. Let us look to the Empire, but remember, too, how much the Scotch are of the *greatness* of *Great* Britain.

HOTEL IN EDINBURGH   Friday

THE City of Edinburgh is a great city for journalists.

You do not meet them, as you meet them in Fleet Street, in one or other of the bars or public houses or eating houses. They are more exiguous figures. They have to be tracked down in their lairs, or accosted on the fringe of committee meetings or detained as they make their way from St. Andrew's House or the Regional Commissioner's Office back to their headquarters.

To-night, however, I have been more fortunate. At a dinner given to one of these many peripatetic missions which come to Edinburgh to see Scotland and all its works, I had the good fortune to be seated next to J. W. Herries, Chief Reporter of the *Scotsman,* I learned from the head waiter. He has quite a pursuing look and if ever a man could be described as having a nose for the reportable I think, seeing him in profile at any rate, Herries is just such an one. He was easily more interesting than the principal guest—in fact more interesting than the whole mission put together and multiplied by ten. What a range that man has, how I envy him the breadth, width and depth of his career! He is a canoeist; he is a member of the Edinburgh Arts Club and knows a great deal about art; he is a Spiritualist and believes not so much in the life to come but the life that is here already, had we but eyes to see it. He is probably right. He did a remarkable play with a background of the last war and is the author, among other books, of an excellent autobiography—"I came, I saw"—and apparently modestly leaves the third assertion "I conquered" to others . . . but he has conquered all right, conquered himself, conquered his medium, conquered his circumstances, and sits serene, Chief Reporter to the *Scotsman*.

(He is a house planner and has adapted a large house as his personal solution to the housing problem of the city.)

He did me a service by defining "love." Apparently one of the Gifford Lecturers (I think he said the name was Caird) defined it as follows: and I copy it from the pencilled note he gave me. . . . "Love," he quoted, "is that identification or confusion of the real with the ideal, of the particular with the general which beauty suggests." There are other journalists—I must collect them, not as butterflies, but as a substantial contribution to this mosaic of mine which I begin to see this diary is becoming.

HOTEL Monday

"EDINBURGH's a good place."

I looked interrogatively. "A good city—morally—ethically—socially—architecturally—which?"

"Neither," he said. "It's a good place for books."

I am grateful to him, my good companion in Room 248 in the hotel. He is some kind of an insurance manager, but that is only incidentally. He may inspect branches or check balances or organize business in some way, but he really comes to Edinburgh for books.

It is a good book town. Printing, paper, education, Sir Walter Scott, Robert Louis Stevenson—all these, I take it, play their part.

Frank truancy it was as far as I am concerned. We left the hotel and went to Elliot's—a thriving bookshop like a W. H. Smith or a Wyman's bookshop—and then, round the corner, into George Street. Brown's—an antique bookshop—and Orr's and Brunton's—all these are bookshops of character—a character which I have not discovered anywhere else.

We came into Princes Street again to see Macniven's shop and then Grant's—which claims to be the oldest bookshop in Scotland. It seemed to me very modern. In a side street is Douglas and Foulis—a wonderful library bookshop—and from there we went to tea.

I was for going back to the hotel—I have work to do, I argued, but my companion of Room 248 would have none of it.

"The best is yet to be," he asserted, and so, up the Mound, past Bauermeister and William Hodge and another one, the name of which I forget, on to John Grant . . . surely the best remainder and second-hand bookshop there is. Then on to James Thin—as real a centre of culture as the University which it adjoins.

"There are more," he said. "You should see Baxendine's." I was firm. "Baxendine for another day, I must go back to my files."

What a delightful pilgrimage among the bookshops. There is nothing like it in any town.

Steady! I must restrain myself. I am *not* going to retire to Edinburgh. I am going back to London.

HOTEL Tuesday

WAR is a serious business for ageing gentlemen who had expected to spend the years of 1940 to 1945 in judicious retirement, lingering over lobelias, garnering geraniums, plucking primroses and, in due season, sucking strawberries.

It is an understatement to admit that I am disappointed by the turn of affairs. The war has been markedly inconvenient to me. It has brought glory and greatness, sacrifice and suffering to countless thousands. As an ageing man whose life has been challenged, I restrain my bitterness, if only out of seemliness.

None the less, in the hotel to-day—the meeting was not until three and luncheon was prolonged—there was a discussion between us as to what we missed most in war time. I did not tell them that I missed most a decent, orderly retirement, a planned progress to the grave, an agreeable dallying in a garden until I must leave it for the crematorium. . . . I did not confess these things because I was amazed at the minor inconveniences of the rest of the party.

"I miss my car most," said one. "I miss my golf," said another. "I miss the chance of getting proper exercise"—"I hate the war because I must sleep with the curtains drawn and get no proper ventilation in my room"—"I hate the war because I cannot get foreign travel"—"I hate the war because I planned to see my granddaughters in New Zealand"—"I hate the war because Havana cigars have been stopped, whisky is practically unobtainable"—"I hate the war. . . ."

As I walked up Cockburn Street to the City Chambers for the meeting at a quarter to three I thought I was a better man. I hate the war because it has destroyed my peace but, please God, with the help of this diary, not my peace of mind.

EDINBURGH Wednesday

THERE are critics of the British Council but here in Edinburgh I find it well presented. Sir Malcolm Robertson and

Mr. Harvey Wood conspire to give the citizens an exhibition of what Jugoslavia has done and I hear of its heroes and its poets, especially its poets.

He is a great writer (I missed his name) no doubt, and is sure of fame, but is it not an exaggeration to claim for him "loftiness" and "sublimity" and "eloquence" and "harmony"?

Isn't it rather overdoing it?

Can poetry have these things and have them recognized by ordinary mortals?

To-night I am emphatically of the opinion that it is overdone, the eulogy. Mine is a more acceptable thing. I am attuned to the simpler ear; the appreciation of the discriminating but yet ordinary man. Proof—of course! I have a postal order for twelve and six "With the Editor's Compliments" for my "most stirring sonnet."

As I sat on the platform, precariously near the edge, crowded out and almost over by the Great Ones of Art and Commerce and Municipal Government, I nursed my little triumph.

I am all eager for next week's issue to see my sonnet in print.

What is Jugoslavia to me when I am to have a sonnet published?

What are the great poets of Jugoslavia to me? Exactly nothing, I regret to write, for I cannot yet recall his name and I had intended to enter it in this book.

HOTEL, EDINBURGH — Thursday

It is to be counted a great good fortune that war has taken me to Scotland. The English know Scotchmen—the exported brand—but they don't know Scotland.

I hope with all the talk of a neglected Colonial Empire, Scotland will not be overlooked. It has immense potentialities. It will be asked, "Why don't the Scotch then develop their own heritage?"

There are many answers. The easy one is that, with England not only a better heritage but a less difficult one to develop, the temptation is irresistible to the more restless and energetic of these northern brethren of ours . . . and there is the old temptation to raid and loot—over the border and home again. There's a lot in that historic practice which explains the Scot, whether on foray in England or further afield in Calcutta, Singapore or Shanghai.

These Scots too, the adventuring sort, play a part in Scotland when they come home again. These neat estates, well developed farms and country houses here and there are monuments to those who went to seek fortune but come home at last to the land of their forbears. I have seen it in the borders—the Burma lot there; in Ayrshire, the Shanghai ones; round Aberdeen, the Indian and Ceylon men . . . they play a part in making Scotland.

I wish there were more.

They don't all come home, I incidentally remind myself. Some Scotchmen find fame and nothing else in the far country. Are there many now in Scotland, or anywhere, who remember John Davidson?

Born in 1857, a clerk in the thread business in Glasgow, he ended his own life over the cliffs in Cornwall. He wrote his own epitaph,

> "Deeds all done and songs all sung,
> While others chant in sun and rain,
> Heel and toe from dawn to dusk,
> Round the world and home again."

Home again—but not to Scotland.

EDINBURGH OFFICE Friday

THE Lord Provost of Edinburgh is quite a collector of Churchilliana. He has, of course, all his Master's works, including the somewhat scarce "Savrola," which I often think resembles young Disraeli's "Popanilla." He has a copy of "Arms and the Covenant"—the speeches from 1928 to 1938 duly signed by the Prime Minister and also by Randolph S. Churchill, his son, who, in the Preface announces he had his father's consent to compile the book. There are many interesting things in the book but one clever thing. The dedication is "To My Father, without whose help this book could never have been written."

That is Randolph rather than Winston, I would aver, but Winston would laugh, I am sure.

Another book in the collection is "Winston Spencer Churchill," by A. MacCallum Scott, dated 1905. In the chapter "A Future Leader?" I found and noted these words—

"He plays for high stakes, but his nerve is steady and his eye clear. He will at any rate make a fight for it, and the fight will be something to have lived for and to have seen."

"To have seen"—MacCallum Scott didn't live to see the fight with mortal eyes. He was killed, so Darling told me, in an aeroplane accident in America.

It is a pity!

I sometimes wish that Jonas Gatterall had lived. He thought me, in his indulgent way, a young man who would go far.

It is true, if travelling is going far I have achieved his highest expectations. How I dislike trains these days!

EDINBURGH Monday

THIS is the anniversary of my father's death. It is strange how lives so close at the beginning are so widely apart at the end. I only learned of my father's death ten days after it occurred. I was cautiously chasing Germans over the Roulers Ridge . . . got news of his death by telegram and of his burial by letter at one and the same time.

He was over seventy. Life had disappointed him. I flatter myself it will not so deceive me. I have no "great expectations." Life early disclosed itself—I came through Marcus Aurelius and Epictetus to be prepared for the view that there wasn't much in it. My father—born in Victoria's reign—believed that the Crystal Palace was indeed a glittering symbol of that best which was to be quite soon. His disillusionment—albeit unconfessed—was imparted to me and he bequeathed me an advantage which I have always valued. No son had a worthier or more durable patrimony.

Not that I have ever been a pessimist—it would be heresy to suggest that I am among the unbelievers. There was a time when I didn't believe anything. Had I not read Mr. Foote in *The Freethinker*—Grant Allen's "Evolution of the Idea of God"—and Ernst Haekel's "Riddle of the Universe"? But these had their day, and any impression they left on me ceased to be. (I eagerly turned to positivism —not the positivism of Auguste Comte, but the positivism of a healthy man and mind. Belief had no difficulties for me.)

I can believe anything. Nothing is too strange, improbable, wonderful, horrible, miraculous, incredible—nothing is too bad—or too good—to be true! All good things are yours and mine. There is no monopoly capitalism in anything that endures.

Scotland has found a shelter beneath—not upon—the Cross of St. Andrew at his house.

There are disaffected ones there, however—the reading, studying sort—and one of these sceptics—anti-Orr rather than anti-Johnston—directed my attention to Adam Smith, author of "An Inquiry into the Nature and Causes of the Wealth of Nations." I found the following and, as war is the time for courage and daring, dare to recall what this great Scotch Philosopher and Economist said on this subject. "In some parts of Lancashire it is pretended that bread of oatmeal is a heartier food for labouring people than wheaten bread. I have frequently heard the same doctrine in Scotland."

Here comes the heresy. "The common people of Scotland who are fed with oatmeal are in general neither so strong nor so handsome as the same rank in England, who are fed with wheaten bread. They neither work so well nor look so well."

I said, "Why not send that to your national newspaper, the *Scotsman*?" Civil servants never dispute policy with their Ministers, I was informed. For my single self, porridge and herring have their place. Porridge with cream is best to my taste and herrings in their kippered incarnation are acceptable, but those Scotsmen—you may hand them the bottle and make them drink, but eating is a different affair. It will want more than education—it will want hard necessity, no equal alternative, good—nay, very good—cooking, convincing arguments from the dieticians—these and more before those comfort-accustomed Scots give up the habits which prosperity has brought to them since they left their cabins and Highland Glens.

It is difficult to give up luxury; some historians say it is impossible for a nation.

GREAT KING STREET, EDINBURGH Friday

HOPE, it has been said, is the redeemer of the world.

It is true. It redeems the world for Mrs. Duguid, who does for me in these grim, north-side Edinburgh lodgings.

Her man died as a result of the wounds he collected on the Somme in 1916—she literally carries on. No ideal state will offer her any easement of her burdens. She cannot rest from her labours for her works do follow her—nay, more, they all but tread her down. She never succeeds in avoiding work. She cannot refuse it.

At five she is stirring. On my white nights I hear her out and about and she is away to office cleaning at six. At eight she is in her house again and produces my coffee. Scotch folk don't as a rule understand coffee. They think it has an infusional capacity equal to tea. They think it goes, in fact, by teaspoonsful. Mrs. Duguid knows better. She takes tablespoonsful—and lavish at that—and so I have a brew which banishes headache and makes up for all the jarrings of the night—makes a new world and me brave enough to face it.

Hope is her quality—not a shadowy thing—but still not a bodied hope. I am headachey—"things will brighten up," declares Mrs. Duguid. Her rheumatism bothers her—it will be better later on in the day. The weather—the war—the wardens—the bombs—the boarders—the busybodies—they will pass—hope justifies her every time. . . . She believes in the cloud with the silver lining, the rainbow's promise, the promises of the parson and politician. She has hope unconsumable, inexhaustible; she is for me the perfect pattern in an unredeemed and, to me, often hopeless prospect.

HOTEL IN EDINBURGH Thursday

At the conference I nodded over—partly from lack of food and partly from having had a bad night.

I was all but asleep.

Harrison—over a cup of tea—sympathized. "You are doing too much, my friend. You will die of King's Cross to Waverley and your epitaph will be 'All Change Here.' "

I smiled feebly, but at dinner we met again—dinner where, these days there's little to learn (from the men) and little to eat, he returned to the subject. "Sleeplessness is a bad habit. You must acquire good habits. Good habits are essential to the good civil servant if he desires to be other than a temporary one—if he desires, in short, to do his country lasting good."

I acquiesced.

"In the early days of the Ministry of Labour, I took to insomnia, but I cured myself by studying it. Some, I admit, ignore it and it passes away, but my mind doesn't work that way."

I acquiesced once again, sleepily this time, and fingered my coffee cup with an air of finality.

Harrison put his hand to his breast and took out a pocket book. I thought the folded paper might be some sleeping draught powder. It wasn't. It contained a number of quotations about sleep—some written but mostly typed.

"Take it, and with it take sweet repose," he said, and was off to his room.

I look at his remedy for sleeplessness now—he did apply his mind to the subject and no mistake.

Swinburne heads the first page:

"Life is a watch or a vision
Between a sleep and a sleep."

Wordsworth tells me:

"Our birth is but a sleep and a forgetting. . . ."

A disturbing observation I felt, for one who forgot, among other things, his umbrella on the train from Purley last Monday forenoon!

But there are others. Cervantes puts into Sancho Panza's mouth the best of the lot. . . .

"Blessings light on him who first invented sleep: it covers a man like a cloak—is meat for the hungry—drink for the thirsty—heat for the cold and coolness for the heated ones. . . ."

Harrison has done the State some service. It is the best White Paper I have read and it sends me back to Shakespeare.

"Sleep that knits up the ravell'd sleeve of care"—and—through Pepys and Shakespeare—"so to bed"—and

"Our little life is rounded with a sleep."

OFFICE, EDINBURGH Friday

SHE is possibly the best secretary in St. Andrew's House, but she doesn't know it. She is, like me, only temporary, and does this not because she wants to but because it is her job in the war. She was in what she thinks was big business, but I know it was a very potty concern. But I don't contradict her because she has that capacity of glorifying all that she does. Her twopenny-halfpenny boss, before she came to St. Andrew's House, is her hero. She has gilded him, embroidered him, glorified him, and I have resisted the temptation to tell her that he did not mean very much anyway.

I have resisted it for good reasons. I am a prudent,

calculating man, I reflect. I know that she will be taken in with me as she was taken in with her previous employer. The urge to gild, embroider, which she practised upon him will be practised with more skill upon me. I will be glorified by her when the war is over. She will talk about me, how wonderful I was, what a contrast I am to all other civil servants whom she meets in the lift or jostles in the corridors. I don't destroy her illusions. I cultivate them. She is co-existent with my self-esteem. She sees me without spot or blemish; she will present me faultless; what a jewel, how priceless, how invaluable.

How wise and discriminating am I to recognize it.

One should preserve such innocence. I cannot, dare not, disillusion her. What a blow it would be for her—and for me—if she only knew!

HOTEL, EDINBURGH — Sunday

THE Scotch take their pleasures sadly and perhaps it is not surprising. It is a sad city, a city of gloom, a sad prospect . . . at least so I felt this Sunday evening at six.

I was told in the lounge of the hotel (a place less suitable for lounging I can hardly imagine, but there it is, it is so described!) all about "Sunday Night at Seven."

"Sunday Night at Seven" is held in a large, round hall, generously donated to the citizens of Edinburgh by one of its great brewers. The beneficence of the brewers is not sufficiently esteemed; the creation of a few Barons seems inadequate recompense for many millions of barrels!

This hall is circular in shape, with a round dome, and I may be wrong about it being the gift of a generous brewer—it may have been a whisky donor, but it was the product of some national fluid, and this building encases, enshrines, envelopes, encloses "Sunday Night at Seven." It is an entertainment provided mainly for the troops, but is supported, too, by large numbers of civilians. They tell me there are 3000 people all comfortably seated. No smoking is allowed. A colleague of the redoubtable Lord Provost is the Impresario, Bailie Adam Miller, a Socialist who finds sociability as near as he can get, being a practical man, to the Socialism of his youth. Bands play on its platform, singers sing; there is sometimes, even, dancing, and there is a brilliant compére. All around is a war atmosphere. They have "God Save The King" and they sing "Abide with me" or some other hymn. There is a hearty heartiness, a joyousness, an abandon about the whole business which is creditable. No merely Civic effort I ever saw had such a spontaneity, such generosity of response to the performers, such gush.

At the end, as a distinguished visitor . . . no one seemed even to know my name . . . I had some tea. The ladies of the Corporation apparently preside—and with what grace and friendliness!

I came home in the October darkness feeling that though bombs may separate, the black-out brings us closer together and whether it was the spirit of the generous donor of the hall in which these festivities were held, I don't know, but I hummed to myself the immortal ballad of the Froth-blowers—"The More we are together the Happier we shall be."

HOTEL AT KING'S CROSS Monday

"You are off to bed?" I agreed. "You don't mind the barrage?" he queried. "I do mind it, but it does not help,"

I replied. I didn't tell him I had got a dirty second-hand copy of "Diary of a Nobody." I bought it just outside King's Cross Station at the shop next the cinema. The book is really dirty. I rubbed it briskly on the lining of my overcoat and clambered up to my room with a sense of triumph—and sanctuary.

King's Cross is—near enough—the district of the immortal Pooter. George Grossmith will be gratified in the Heavenly Places (in which he is entitled to dwell) to know that his book was balm to the bombed. He could not have imagined such an excellent posterity, but he will be saddened to think that Mr. Pooter's house and that of his neighbours and, too, his London have largely been destroyed.

My friend Blair couldn't enjoy "Diary of a Nobody." I enthused about it. I praised it. I pressed it on him. I told him Lord Rosebery, not the Regional Commissioner but the Orator, had written that, in his view, no bedroom was properly furnished without it. He took the book.

He handed it back to me the following Sunday. I asked him what he thought of it. He replied, "It is too sad."

He was right in his wise, reflective way. Human life is sad. All diaries are sad. Samuel Pepys in the end came to blindness. Edward Gibbon laid down his writing, which had been his dear companion, with more than a sigh. There is so much to write and it is of so little account, for has it not all been said before? "As it was written."

EDINBURGH AT THE OFFICE Wednesday

SCOTLAND has about five millions and for their number

they are a pertinacious people. To-day I learn there are thirty-five million Poles. How much more fortunate have the Scotch been with their neighbours than the Poles! We English don't expect much but, truth to tell, the Scotch, Welsh, and Irish have not been easy bedfellows. Of the lot, the Scotch have been least trouble, but they have exacted their price. We had to take their James VI after beheading his mother, and they have tried to put it across us ever since. No wonder, I reflected. They think if we would take King Jamie, "the wisest fool in Europe," we would take anything.

It is true. We are allergic (is that the word? I ought to carry a dictionary in my satchel) to the Scotch. We always give them a good place. "Scotty" is always played up by the English. Some of us are jealous. For a small people we have given them a due share in the partnership. Ernest Brown told a meeting of Scotsmen to-day that the Prime Minister had said that there was one fault about Scotland. The meeting gasped. What a heresy! One fault in Scotland—that was incredible. Mr. Ernest Brown reassured them: "The fault of Scotland," it was alleged the Prime Minister had said, "is that there are too few Scotsmen."

They were happy. My neighbour wrote on his menu card, "Wha's like us? De'il a yin."

I copy it out now. I copy it out carefully. I reflect he let me take it reluctantly. The Scotchman wanted to keep the card and what he had written on it for himself!

EDINBURGH Thursday

THEY come among us increasingly. They are deceptively like us because they speak the tongue that Shakespeare spoke. They have Scotch and English names. They claim origins in this island. They have ancestors here: they have roots.

It is very deceptive and therein lies a danger. We accept them too readily as understanding us—and we, them—but it is not as it appears. Americans are foreigners. Their way of life isn't ours. They ride horses in Texas. They chew gum in New York. They drink universally a beverage called "Coke." They call any woman who looks young enough "Sister." With them things are "Okay"—and the affirmative is "Yep" and the negative "Nope."

Well, well.

They are really a democratic people and we really are not a democratic people. They are dedicated to the proposition that all men are equal. We know better. We have lived longer. Democracy is not an English thing. The English heritage is surely that men are individual . . . that men are equal only in the mystical eyes of God.

Democracy belonged to a people who knew Demos as their divinity. We have only learned about him in our classical text books. We didn't enthrone him. We still believe in the divine rights of Kings—and of ordinary men.

This is a stratified society and with all its changes—all its extensions and faults—it still remains stratified.

"Yes, sir," he says to me with emphasis on the sir—but it's not respect. It is a strident assertion of an equality he doubts and over emphasizes because he doubts.

I am not greatly concerned. When they are through with this second World War—well, they will have learned the second part of their lesson. We are higher up in the class.

EDINBURGH Friday

WOMEN are the ones; I would like to invent a new word and write that women are the "wones."

This Civil Defence business is theirs. They know that the woman's place is the home and they will defend the home at all cost and regardless of expenditure of time, labour, and money.

They are right. Privately, the world would have finished but for the women. A birth-strike in the Ice Age would have burst the Divine purpose.

But they went on with it; "it" being the business of food and drink and caves and shelter and babies and reluctant males as hunters.

These planners of a new society should look at it again, their background. Kent's Cavern down at Torquay should be visited by deputations from every planning authority; it ought to be a National Monument—and a warning.

Life didn't begin yesterday.

The women know the facts.

I hope the days are over when they are carried away by the men. They are no longer physically so transported, but it is their mental portability that concerns me. The only cure for the careless raptures of the sex is the homœopathic one. If women are interested in politics introduce them to a woman Member of Parliament.

There is an end to all things, they say!

Was Dumas cruel or cynical when he wrote—

"The Bible says that woman is the last thing that
God made.
He must have made it on Saturday night.
It shows fatigue."

LONDON, AT HOME Saturday

How changed is this world of London after weeks in Edinburgh. I don't like it. I think I will settle in Edinburgh after the war. The rates are low, the Lord Provost told me—he has told me more than once!

But to-night I have a sense of expectation. It would be too bad if I get killed in London when I am posted to Scotland. But I don't like the moon. I don't like it.

You would have been welcome once. Dogs would have had vocal exercise and bayed at you. Lovers would have walked under your beams in ridiculous but, fortunately, transitory ecstasy; old folks walking home from dinner parties would have agreed that it was a fine moonlit night. Not so, now.

Grubby wardens, grim rescue and repair men, experienced police officers, high officials in the Air Ministry, pundits of the press, even members of the staff of the Ministry of Information . . . all look anxiously toward the clear heavens where you reign alone. They will be over to-night, they say.

One day will come, however, when you will be welcome again.

One day I will say, "Yes, let it be Tuesday. We will come that evening. It will be full moon. I always enjoy a walk on a moonlit night."

Yes, one day I will say it.

It will not be to-night. Shall I undress or lie down on the bed as I am? How many ask that question to-night? How many ask it and won't ask it to-morrow? It is a little devastating.

I will calm myself by reading my official papers.

How dull they are.

They will soothe, however.
They will effectively emphasize the futility of things.
They always do.

HOME Sunday

"When wilt thou save the people?
Oh, God of Mercy! when?
The people, Lord, the people!
Not thrones and crowns—but men!"

Ebenezer Elliott, a distant ancestor of mine, if my Mother is to be believed, wrote that. The goodness of the ordinary man makes me humble.

Frankly, I marvel. What is he anyway? For years unemployed—a discard of society, nursing his impaired lungs with no resentment for the poison gas which damaged them, with no hatred for the system which has denied him a maintenance in exchange for a life more than half broken in its service on the battlefield, he now fulfils loyally his function.

His is Wardens' Post "C," but he is the post itself. Without him the half-hearted would not be there; without him the enthusiastic would fail in their devotion. He is the Post—and when trouble comes, as it has come—he is there to lead if there are any to lead, but to do if his is alone the responsibility.

Whence comes this marvel?

There is no ready answer but I am persuaded that he draws his strength unknown to him from the veritable wells of Creation. He is rooted in the very foundations of things. His contempt of danger is of a piece with eternal law which, from the beginning, knows that all things work together for good and in the last resort all is well.

There are resolutions to do better, to make plans. Resolutions will be resolved in action and plans in performance, but I hope we won't forget the ordinary man. He is worth all we can give him. I hope I won't forget. I hope we will all remember.

HOTEL, EDINBURGH Tuesday

How many are the definitions of happiness? The quality or condition of being happy, says the dictionary, but there are wider boundaries. It is fortunate so. The Happy Isles have a diversified and undiscriminating population. A walk along the main street discloses many happy people.

Small boy scouts tugging at a truck. A mother with parcels and two children and a face aglow, on the way to the railway station. A civil servant with his black, monogrammed satchel bending his way to St. Andrew's House to settle the problems of hill sheep. The hotel porter, spruce, well groomed, distinguished, available to serve and serve alone apparently without hope or expectation of reward; these seem to me happy people. My eyes lift from the present scene. The enigma of life invades me. Life, liberty and the pursuit of happiness—these are man's rights. Life and liberty are the tangibles. They can be had and held, but not so happiness. Happiness is in the pursuit, not the attainment. Happiness cannot be held, it can only be sought for, run after, chased, hunted, searched for; it can only be pursued and the right to pursue is all.

Pursuit does not, fortunately, imply haste. It may come to the idler as readily as to the ardent hunter. It may be at one's doorstep as surely as at the end of the world. I am certain of that as I enjoy one of my few remaining Havana cigars, sitting in this bare writing room in what once was called a luxury hotel.

Happiness comes indiscriminatingly. It does not respond to invitation. It ignores being ignored. It is a law unto itself but I can find its laws in no books.

OFFICE, LONDON — Thursday

THE British Restaurants are well named. British to me means barbarian. They are barbarian, brutal in their cooking, brutal in their presentation of food. One needs to be British "to take it" in a British Restaurant.

To-day, appropriately, in the British Restaurant, I met a Chinaman. He tells me strange tidings. Do I know Sinkiang? No, I don't. This place is a north-western province in China. It is the hub of the world for Russia. Sheng Shih-tzai is its President. He is a reformer. He has made a new country, with much wealth and power. His people are electrically minded, they have national wireless and films. They are strongly affiliated to the U.S.S.R. and accept their economics and politics.

And the Chinaman tells me all about Sinkiang and I know nothing, have heard nothing, about it. Do the Foreign Office know? Does the place authentically exist or am I just a gossiping Roman legionary hearing strange tales from a comrade in what I think is a British Fort, but what really is a British Restaurant?

What do any of us know of the war—the world—if you like? Where is this security of which Beveridge bleats? The world—life—these are incurably mysterious and adventurous. They are better so. The Civil Service, in spite of

Sir Warren and Sir Horace and Sir Richard, can never make things civilized, far less civil.

There is an untamed wildness in which with all my seven pairs of neat striped trousers I secretly rejoice. I know the British Restaurants are well named. To be British—is to be barbarian. To be a Civil Servant is a pose. I have neither civility nor servility.

AT THE OFFICE, LONDON Friday

THE City of London is sadly ravaged these days. Pepys wouldn't have liked it, neither would John Evelyn. I wonder if there are diarists of their quality making notes to-day of what they see around them for the enlightenment of to-morrow?

The dust and disorder around me made me turn into a church. For the life of me I cannot remember its name now but it is near Moorgate Street. I will go there again. I feel I found peace there for an hour. The parson didn't come up to my expectations but, as I sat, a benevolence came over me.

We are not fair to parsons. Theirs is a high, a lofty, a difficult calling. They do their best, I felt, as I sat in that musty atmosphere. None of us has such a high standard as they. They have to make the case for goodness, the case for God.

My task is trifling by comparison. I make the case for my Minister but he may be gone to-morrow, or, if he stays, the decisions are his and his failings are his own. The parson has to justify God's ways to man not for this Parliament but from everlasting to everlasting; not for to-day but for eternity.

Let us then not be too hard on the parsons. Theirs is a hard road and a broken road in the city, any way, to-day. It must have been feelings like these that made me put two half crowns in the box as I left.

Voluntary collections are right. Auberon Herbert advocated voluntary taxation. His idea was that the State should get what the taxpayers thought it was worth to them. What an idealist that man was! But in the last resort is not Anarchy the only freedom?

HOME Saturday

A FREQUENT fellow sojourner on the King's Cross-Edinburgh train is Ernest Brown.

The Right Honourable Ernest Brown, M.C., M.P., preacher, orator, politician, soldier, statesman; he told me he has "ministered" to us—as a Minister—for over ten years. It was an understatement; he has done more than any other Minister—more—that is—continuously. I think he has done it well. In conference he compares favourably with many of his colleagues. He has, of course, vast experience. He reads his papers, too—he knows his brief. He can put a case over, as they say, in the House of Commons as well as any, and it would be for him—I fancy—the highest felicity to be called "a first-class House of Commons man."

He is one of the fighting men in the Government. There are not so many. Eden and Brown both have the Military Cross—and so has "Shakespeare" Morrison. There may be more, but it is not invariable for valour on the field of battle to be matched with courage in the Cabinet. Many can make a fighting speech—not so many have done the fighting as well as the speaking.

I feel grim to-night—perhaps it's the news of the war. In the last resort courage is all. Courage for the citizen—courage for the statesman—courage for the soldier—so I reflect.

And it is the Right Honourable Ernest Brown, M.C., M.P., who suggests these reflections. He has courage. He is, I sense it, essentially a fighting man—whether it is at Ypres or Leith, at St. Stephens or St. Andrew's House or with U.N.R.A. We will want Ernest in days to come. We will need him, perhaps it is more accurate to say—and it will be our loss if we don't want him and his like.

OFFICE, LONDON Monday

WORDSWORTH as a prophet for these days has a useful place. I find it lightens the day's urgency, and the day's vast futility, to have his assurance that "our birth is but a sleep and a forgetting." We are enfranchised of futurity. We come from afar. We need not regret the littleness of life. There is more to come. We mock at the thoughts of dissolution. Ours is the amplitude of time. These are, of course, personal consolations. The same Wordsworth has less comfort for Herr Hitler this morning.

If he is reading—which I must confess is unlikely—Wordsworth's Sonnets dedicated to Liberty, he will find no happy fate presaged for him. I read:

"Look now on that adventurer who hath paid
His vows to fortune—who in cruel slight
Of virtuous hope, of liberty and right
Hath followed wheresoe'er a way was made."

What is his fate? I console myself for a much disturbed night and a disarranged morning. Here is his fate.

"Him"—that adventurer—"from that height shall
Heaven precipitate
By violent and ignominious death."

It is little enough. The plumbing of the whole block of flats is sadly out of order. They dig in the street below. It is little enough.

I reiterate.

Wordsworth never felt so deeply as some of us after a night of bombing.

EDINBURGH IN THE MORNING — Wednesday

My journey back to Edinburgh was a sombre one. There was no sleeper so I sat up in a first rather than recline in the third offered to me. The journey was sombre because of my parting from Jelk.

Jelk, I used to think, was one of the fortunate ones. He did well in the war and came through, and the Baldwin days found him high in favour. He suited that atmosphere more than I did, and now he is on his way out and almost knows the date.

In the nursing home at Streatham (why he has gone to Streatham I didn't ask—I would sooner have had it out in St. Thomas), he told me that all the vagueness and delicacy of the surgeon and the doctors had not concealed from him the fact that his days in the land were numbered.

What consolation can one offer? What can one say?

As I walked over Streatham Common I cursed myself for my wordlessness; I who thought I had the gift of language could find no words to express my thoughts and during the sleepless, sordid journey none have come. I want to write to him, but what can I write? Years ago I read a book, "The Journal of a Disappointed Man." It was anonymous or under a pseudonym anyway, and the writer, too, was under a sentence of death. He found courage in himself. He threw away self-pity. He denied himself even stoicism and self-resignation. He fought it out to the last. There is little guidance in this business of dying, of "getting cleanly off the stage."

It is one of the few things we don't know how to plan. It is always unexpected, it seems to me, and they are not so unfortunate, those who are taken unawares. To cease upon the midnight with no pain; how happy are they who have that fortune.

My Uncle Bill had a book on his shelves, it stood next to Stephens's Book of the Farm, I remember, called "Holy Living and Holy Dying"—but I was of no mind in those days to read it; and now I cannot find it. Plato, I have, however.

"Let a man be of good cheer about his soul, who has cast away the pleasures and ornaments of the body as alien to him and has followed after the pleasures of knowledge in this life, who has adorned the soul in her own proper jewels, which are temperance and justice and courage and nobility and truth."

That might do for Jelks except that he has Plato more than I. The conclusion of the whole matter is resignation. "And so I betake myself to my grave," said Samuel Pepys at the end of the diary, "to see myself into my grave—for which the Good God prepare me."

HOTEL IN EDINBURGH Thursday

EDINBURGH is a city of philosophers. You see them on

sunny mornings in Princes Street, peering at bookshops, holding bags and parcels for their shopping wives as they loiter on the kerbs of the pavement, walking smartly into the University Club or strolling along to the Northern Club, an ivy covered residence which I have discovered in George Street in this city.

Philosophers are not all university men in Edinburgh. There are fewer there than I had expected. Edinburgh has a number of famous professors, and curiosity took me to the Reference Library in George IV Bridge to look up the University Calendar. Two distinguished names caught my eye, the names of John Dover Wilson and Thomas Holland.

Dover Wilson has brought Shakespeare to the City of Edinburgh. I see his book on Falstaff showing in the bookshops and I am told that he has given public lectures on his subject. Shakespeare, I remind myself, was my passion last war with Frank Harris's "The Man, Shakespeare" as my handbook. Professor Masson, surely an Edinburgh man too, has a book "Shakespeare Personally" and is a not inferior second. Since then I have wandered from my books and Shakespeare is, more or less, from a reading point of view, now a memory. But Dover Wilson's name reminded me of this well of English undefiled from which we still may draw so copiously. I asked an Edinburgh colleague about Dover Wilson, and he told me he lived outside Edinburgh, although he lectured in the University. "A remarkable man," I was told, and I readily believe it; but more than that he has his great work on Shakespeare to complete, I am informed. His relaxation is reading Anthony Trollope and he has bought a complete set—so my gossip tells me. It stands on his mantleshelf, a long row of small volumes. As he reads each volume he removes its "jacket." Anthony Trollope was a civil servant—an Inspector of Post Offices, and his leisure for writing must have been scanty as he rode his horse round England and Ireland inspecting his post offices, yet he made thousands by writing books. I don't know which appeals to me the more, making thousands or writing books. I am not so greedy as to want both; how happy I would be with either!

EDINBURGH Friday

LAST night my entry was about Edinburgh University and I come back to it again because I have taken a turn through its quadrangle and on an earlier occasion I have seen its scattered buildings, like a model factory, on the south side of the City near Blackford Hill.

Dover Wilson is only one of Edinburgh's celebrated professors. The Principal of the University is also a national—nay, an international figure, the redoubtable Thomas Holland, Fellow of the Royal Society. He seemed to me to be one of the most practical men who applied themselves to the problems of world peace before the present war. He is a geologist, a man of affairs; he indicated what were the essential war-making minerals, where they were located, in what quantities they existed, put forward a practical proposal for League of Nations control of these essential materials to reduce the chances of war—at any rate on a mammoth scale—if not entirely remove them. If Holland had had his way, the peoples of the world would still have fought, no doubt—such is the incorrigible obstinacy of mankind, but they would have had to fight with pikes such as Lord Croft recommended to the Home Guard, or even, in better days, would have recognized that the pen is mightier than the sword and used it as their most lethal weapon.

It was not to be. Sir Thomas Holland's counsel was not accepted, although not unacceptable, but we might have another chance. Sir Thomas Holland's choice as the Principal of the University of Edinburgh surely was remarkable. He has no claims to any Scottish connexion. His life had been spent, largely, in India where he did very notable public service in the fields of administration, production and finance, and it is said that when he was asked to Edinburgh he did not know which of the many Edinburghs was referred to in the cable which reached him somewhere in South America! That I can hardly believe, but the high authority in the smoking room is emphatic in asserting its truth. There are, in fact, over thirty Edinburghs or variations of Edinburgh such as Dunedin, and perhaps the uncertainty was not so much in the mind of Sir Thomas Holland as in the minds of those who were responsible for handing him the invitation which he subsequently accepted to become Principal of the University of the City of Edinburgh.

Principals of Edinburgh University have, in the main, been scientific. His immediate predecessor, Sir Alfred Ewing, was an engineer, and before that, I believe, a physician, which is all the more remarkable in that Edinburgh, famous for its Medical School, is also no less famous for its humanities. Oliver Goldsmith joins hands over the years with James Matthew Barrie; R.L.S. and Sir Walter Scott are also of the company, but perhaps it is true that the arts are best learned under the auspices of the sciences.

It is perhaps my defect that I have not such an admirable intellectual background as the fortunate students of Edinburgh either advertently or inadvertently secure.

Perhaps.

LONDON Saturday

"For three good reasons," writes H. A. L. Fisher of Napoleon, "he could not afford to see the Bourbons back in Paris; they would make peace in Europe, they would govern France, and they would certainly dispense with his services."

There are a good many in this war who, like Napoleon, have a vested interest in its continuance, and they are not all soldiers. One does not grudge the opportunity to the soldiers. They have to wait for it: they pay a big price when they are waiting and the best of them go down in the opening months of any war.

I've seen three wars and lost relatives and friends in them all. I was troubled by an In Memoriam in *The Times*. It told of three men—or, rather, two men and a boy—the men found graves in Natal and Belgium, the boy in the Channel in the Battle of Britain. It cannot be exceptional. "If blood be the price of admiralty," England has paid for it—or, rather, English women have paid it.

"They would certainly dispense with his services," makes me think of the politer, the Civil—Service, and its war-time accretions. They have a vested—nay more—a triple-armoured interest.

The Chancellor of the Exchequer, in a written answer, indicates that the number of the non-industrial staffs employed at 1st April, 1943, amounts to 93,680. These, I note, are war-time Ministries: food, fuel, economic warfare, and so on; they do not include the pre-war organization, the Foreign Office, Sir Kingsley's own department, War, Air, Admiralty.

What a picture of a great nation at war! What a picture of limpets, embusqués and hangers-on! What a picture of the clumsiness of the State when it seeks to do anything for its citizens. It almost makes me a member of the Society of Individualists.

It will be a problem to get rid of them all . . . they have a vested interest in war and in bureaucracy, and there is only one consolation. They are not all Napoleons—none of them!

LONDON Monday

NOEL COWARD fills the bill these days. His restless activities shame me, for I have hitherto looked on him as something of a social butterfly. He works as hard as Shakespeare and travels more than ever he did.

It isn't often I get to the theatre now. This office, night work, standing by for what happens or doesn't happen, the black-out, these have broken a theatre-going habit which has been the greatest of the joys of my middle age, but on Saturday I saw Coward in "Blithe Spirit." The man is so much different from the rest of us that I must dub him a genius. His subtlety, his mannerisms, his naturalness—they have all the richness of Restoration Comedy—surely the merriest moment in the history of Merrie England. We dined after the Show. He was full of the dangers of "Careless Talk," of men and women who simply must show that they are in the know by telling what they have gleaned or deduced or even been told. He wants a ban on all that, but he asks for too much from frail humanity.

My idea is more careless and also more careful talk. Let us all talk. We have a new tank with ten torpedoes, a new plane with radio death-rays. We are going to land by parachutes in Berlin or Budapest. We are going to invade the Channel Islands or Crete. Let us all use our imaginations and keep the German agents busy investigating everything. Let them run hither and thither, no tale can be too unlikely to be true, too improbable to ignore; in that way, I said, we will confound their knavish tricks.

I was quite heatedly eloquent about it but Noel Coward was unconvinced. He may be wiser; he is subtler than I.

INVERNESS — Wednesday

YEARS ago I first met him. It must have been in the Somme in 1916. He has done well. He entered the Civil Service as a special entrant and for a long time lived in some almost underground position in one department or another. He married unhappily, I have heard, but he had cleared all that up by 1939. He emerged and Mr. Chamberlain fell, and now, neat, bland, competent, effective, he is a Ruler.

We had to share a bedroom; the accommodation in these remote places because of commandeering imposed this condition on us. He astonished me. His deliberate, careful undressing. His arrangement of his watch, chain, pen, pencil—and—amazing—his silver pocket paper-knife on the dressing table impressed me. He got into his pyjamas. He claimed the bed with the bedside light. I yielded it to him although to read in bed is not the least of my preparations for slumber. I turned my face away from the light towards the wall. He read a long time. I fell asleep. He was still reading. When he went to the bathroom in the morning I looked at the book he had read so faithfully. It was "The Thoughts of Marcus Aurelius Antoninus." The book was worn. Many passages were marked. "What means all this?" It was heavily underlined. "Thou hast embarked. Thou hast made the voyage. Thou art come ashore: get out."

I have discovered his secret. Never again can I feel other than that I understand him. I have a feeling for him. There may be something, after all, in sharing a bedroom with a man, but it was the Emperor Marcus who revealed him.

RAILWAY STATION HOTEL — Thursday

GOOD food in the sense that it appeals to the palate is not possible in war time. A growing experience of hotels, boarding houses, canteens, and private hospitality drives this melancholy conclusion in upon me.

It is sad for, at my age, a good dinner is not to be despised as one of the lesser pleasures of a rapidly concluding existence.

Lord Woolton's devices may have made the nation healthier. They certainly have destroyed its taste.

The place in which I write this sheet has done its best, but herrings for breakfast, fish pie for lunch, and steamed halibut or skate or what not for dinner, leave me sick of the sea and all its finny, slimy products.

It has been left to these later years, the experience of potatoes and margarine as a main dish, and that only as a bitter alternative to what is called "Gnocchi" an Italianate concoction, patriotically marked "V"—the Victory sign—an indication of the victory of necessity over the palate.

Beds are my consolation. Give me a bed and I will give the night porter half a crown for his wholly unconnected association with my good night's rest. All hotel advertisements are incomplete for me in the future, if there is one for me in this Island, unless they indicate that they have GOOD BEDS. If I knew that, I would feel that Christina Georgina Rossetti was more than a poet; her assertion that there are "beds for all who come" would make her a prophetess.

EDINBURGH Friday

FRANKLY, this Savings Meeting has opened a new world for me. There is a whole literature, apparently, of savings, thrift and parsimony, of which I was never aware. Sad women keep pound notes by the hundred under their mattresses, save them in teapots, hide them in the pages of books and, from time to time, they are extracted by the solicitations of those most honourable of street walkers, the endlessly industrious servants of the Savings Movement.

At a Reception given in the City Chambers, I sat apart and heard the story of Hetty Green. Hetty Green was the richest woman in the world and she lived most of her life in cheap boarding houses. She wore the shabbiest of black raiment. She wasn't really a business woman, but was born to wealth. "Never owe anything," her father instructed her, "never owe even a kindness." Apart from her inheritance, which must have been over a million pounds in our money, she was in her own right a financial genius. Her principle was to look for something that was going cheap, something that no one else was buying in the stock market and, having bought it she would put it away and wait for her time. She did a lot in land and property speculation and showed over her career an instinct for investment which was miraculous. Apart from her parsimony, she was quite an average sort of woman, married, had two children; her health, which was excellent, she claimed was due to her practice of eating an onion every day, and it was nothing ordinary that brought about her death. She died, over 80, because of a row she had with her servant.

Such was Hetty Green, and the story was told to me by a housewife who had learned it from somebody in the Library and who had been driven to study Hetty Green because of her interest in the Savings Movement.

How extraordinarily the world fits together. What Sir John Anderson would think of it if he knew the details, I can't imagine, but there are many women padding the hoof, collecting the pounds and studying miserliness, all in the interests of removing the Führer from his position as head of the Third Reich, and there are people who think rationality, sanity, normality are possible things in human relations. The attempt to state a fact is to call for its immediate denial. We are powerfully and wonderfully made.

LONDON, NEW YEAR'S DAY Saturday

MOST New Year's Days have come to me in bed. The habit of the Scotch to see the New Year in, as they call it, has always seemed to me to be the triumph of curiosity over experience. Only the Scotch, perhaps, have reason to hope for the better in the New Year; their Calvinistic souls cry aloud for another chance, another gamble against the predestination that around enmeshes them.

New Year's Day should be spent in quiet reflection. At my duty, I ruminate and recall and regret. The month belongs to Janus—that two-faced deity who looks before and after and, so inspired, I turn to the New Year that begins to-day.

Recollection rules this day for me and the places in which I have spent it; swimming on the coasts of Ceylon, a child at a New Year party, in 1917 down in the Somme battlefields, in 1913 at St. Paul's, hailing 1914, a year charged heavy with fate for millions. . . . I recollect them all, and with them

"The friends so linked together
I've seen around me fall
Like leaves in wintry weather."

But no sadness is in these recollections. God balances His ledgers. We each get our deserts, I am convinced. It is, I admit, an act of faith, but convictions are often best grounded in faith.

Wordsworth, to whom I return, has it in "The Excursion": I am . . .

"One in whom persuasion and belief
Had ripened into faith, and faith become
A passionate intuition."

It is a good approach to this New Year; "a passionate intuition."

LONDON Tuesday

THEY are having talks and conferences about the future of Local Government. They ought to beware. Birmingham doesn't like it. Bristol has its views. These Regional Commissioners—well—as I was asked the other day, "Who are they anyway?"

Frankly, I couldn't answer. In the 1938 period, it was sound to appoint them. Things were not all at the same pitch. Some local authorities said "Air-raid Precautions Act—let it lie on the table"—but now there is a very different story.

This fair but battered land of ours will be wise to hold fast to its Local Government. The parish pump is a more convenient rallying centre for the people than the secret Regional Headquarters. To-day, I have met the Scotchmen, Darling, Biggar, Wilson, Nimmo, and Mitchell, Lord Provosts of Edinburgh, Glasgow, Dundee, Perth, and Aberdeen.

They have a proverb in Scotland: "Wha daur meddle wi' me," and this quintette frankly bristle with defensive and, when needed, offensive words. I do my best with them but confess—but not to them—that my Minister's plans are worsted.

"Worsted"—how odd the significance of words; worsted his plans? They are not worsted, they are woolly, and the Provosts said so.

I fear the Mayors will say the same.

They are not so formidable, however, I have found. These Scotch ones hold office for three years—hold is the word—they are tenacious. The English Mayors, even the Lord Mayor of London, I discover, hold office for one year only; that makes them easier.

LONDON Wednesday

YOUNG CHARLEY I call him; I knew his mother, who did not long survive his father, a Royal Fusilier who lies in Tyne Cot Cemetery beside Ypres. Young Charley has been "grounded" as they call it. These Royal Air Force boys are, of course, a miracle to me as they must be to millions.

From whom do they draw their greatness? From whence do they find their cloak—the camouflage—of boyish innocence with which they, for me, surround themselves? I do not know. They must have access to the well at the world's end, or the waters of eternity.

They elude me.

To Charley, I said, when I had taken him to the play and given him supper, "You must have a souvenir of this night." He didn't want anything. Cigarette case, pipe, torch, gloves, wristlet watch, fountain pen, pigskin leather holdall—he had them all—or didn't want them. "You must have something." "No thanks—I've had a wizard evening." "Here is my card. Go to Bumpus. Choose any book you want except Encyclopædia Britannica."

To-day I've got Charley's bill. He chose "The Oxford Book of Victorian Verse."

My copy, I see, was given me in 1914. It is full of memories, and bitter laughs too. William H. Davies's poem—its first two lines—

"What is this life if full of care
We have no time to stand and stare?".

take me back with a swoop to two days when we waited and waited for an overdue relief from the trenches we held. How different these lines may read to Charley!

LONDON Thursday

SIR THOMAS BROWNE—good man—knowledgeable, thoughtful, wise fellow . . . he wrote:

"Every man is not only himself. Men are lived over again. The world is now as it was in ages past. There was none then, but there hath been some one since, that parallels him, and is, as it were, his revived self."

His revived self—a mere parallel and replica of what has been . . . how sobering a thought that would be to the young major. He told us all in the railway carriage of what he had been and what he had seen of wars and their ways and old Moxon, who was in the South African War and the last war and who bore but did not boast a D.S.O. and two bars on his breast, heard it uncomfortably and with impatience as he sat, one of the two centre places, in the four-a-side company.

A mere parallel; how proud we are—I am—of our little lives and how we imagine they are unique.

The thing that has been is the thing that shall be. History repeats itself, even the historians repeat themselves, even the diarists can find no new days; even I find Sir Thomas Browne has said it all and said it better years and years ago.

But I am not discomfited. The Lord of Life, as G. K. Chesterton has said, may applaud every sunrise and say to the sun "do it again." He may applaud, I think He does, our petty performances and never tires of the stage play of man—in the world—at his work.

LONDON OFFICE Friday

LEAVING the office for the Ministry of Home Security I

met Yoxall. Yoxall should have been a Civil Servant. I think he has all the marks of a good Civil Servant—knowledgeability, patience, understanding, courtesy. . . . Yoxall has all these things and is no Civil Servant. He was one of those young men who were at the University when the last war descended upon them, and when the war was over found themselves heroes, but in a London in which heroes were six a penny and not as highly esteemed as they had been when the demand was large. He went to the United States and is now a Director General of one of the big women's papers—I don't mean a paper for big women, I mean a big paper, a paper which women buy in a big way. He told me that he now lives at Richmond and is chief air-raid warden, while his wife is chief of the local savings movement. He would rather be at the war again, so I thought as we had a drink together in the Constitutional Club. He left me with a delightful picture of himself as a warden, ribbons up, Military Cross and all, in his blue warden's suit which his wife describes as his "rompers."

He has been a great success with the Americans, I am told. And no wonder. He understands them and they understand him. He presents himself to the Americans as the kind of Englishman they expect. He never disappoints those of his countrymen who rely upon him to represent them favourably. What would we have done in this war without the Yoxalls who, in the aggregate, have given the greater part of their daily life to their country's service; soldiers last war, civil defenders this war, and heaven knows which is the more important. I look upon them as typical with their private worries, their carking responsibilities, their limited leisure filled with Civil Defence and Natonal Savings—they are typical of us. If this is an heroic age, it is because we are an heroic people.

I remind myself that Yoxall has written books. I wish I could write a book.

I never leave Yoxall but with a feeling of deficiency. He has, I suppose, the riches of existence quite unconsciously and those who make a sorry shape of things are made conscious, not depressingly conscious, yet conscious, of their shortcomings. A diary should not be a book of personal praise, a diary should be a confessional book.

I confess and blot the page.

HOME Sunday

WE must have our guides, philosophers, and friends in war time. The economy in man power this war has reduced their numbers and it was interesting for me to share the same roof with Professor Joad. He continues the rôles in the 1914-1919 war, of Hilaire Belloc and Horatio Bottomley, and does it well. He is less historical than the first, but commands a greater public than the second, although he is not such a good platform man as the one-time Member for Hackney. I had the curiosity to turn him up in my hostess's "Who's Who" at the very moment we were drinking beer together, or, more accurately, he and I were drinking beer and he only was talking. His Christian name is "Cyril."

Pursuing my studies, while he still talked, in the pages of "Encyclopædia Britannica," I learned about the other famous Cyrils. There are three recorded, two of whom are saints and one the Apostle of the Stars.

The two saints were violently controversial persons and I imagine the Apostle of the Stars even in the ninth century was not without his trials and troubles.

Cyril, then—I mean Cyril Edwin Mitchinson Joad—was given a suitable name at baptism.

I didn't agree with some of the party that he is just a hum-bug. He is a creature of his time as we all are, industrious, courageous. I was impressed but not sufficiently attracted to him to call him Cyril. He will be a brave man who will do that. Joad—just Joad—seems more natural. I wonder why?

OFFICE, WHITEHALL Monday

"I COULDN'T bayonet a man." His father, a permanent assistant secretary, smiled at his offspring and acquiesced. He didn't go to the last war, and mildly—for he is a selfish man—sympathized with his son. He quite understood. He appreciated that his son would be better in the administrative branches of the service.

Hell!

There used to be an academic question when I was in the Fabian Society in the old days: "Who will do the dirty work under Socialism?" The Fabians didn't answer as far as I remember, except by securing jobs which ensured that they didn't do it.

The question of the day, indeed, of the hour, is who is to do the bayoneting—the really bloody business. Freedom must be secured. Righteousness must prevail. A better world must be born, we are all agreed. But who is to blast and bayonet and bomb and blitz the brutes that stand in the way (in our opinion) of these desirable and necessary ends?

Not me, says bureaucrat—not me, says the intellectual—not me, says the planner—not me, say the clergy, the teachers, the professors, the doers of essential war work—not unto us O! Lord! Society must, then, not only tolerate but encourage a class of persons, in no inconsiderable numbers either, who are bold and brutal and, indeed, at times licentious. Its comforts, its plans, nay, its very foundations rest on these.

I must remember that the next time I am crowded into the corridor by the rude soldiery.

I must be meek and gentle—was it Shakespeare who has it?—"with these butchers."

EDINBURGH Tuesday

How unsentimental are my journeys! How strangely lacking in adventure compared with those of Laurence Sterne and he a clergyman too! (Who reads "A Sentimental Journey" to-day?)

King's Cross—the Sleeping Berth office. Yes, there was a berth but the Ministry have cancelled yours—a lady—the Head of the W.V.S.—essential—returning from important conference—must be in Inverness to-morrow night—very sorry.

So it went. I in front of the counter—the glass topped counter—tattered railway guides—behind, telephones, and bright, shiny girls in a blue colourless light—there I received my doom. A night sitting up and I was so tired of London and potato cakes for breakfast. I hungered for Scotland. He was moved by my dejection. He has seen me often, the head booking clerk. "Will you share one?" I inquired further. "We have two-decker Firsts." Hope springs eternal. "Springs" is not the word for this occasion—it gushed. "Can you give me one?" I ploughed away with my snatchel—a better word than satchel—and found these double-deckers. How little room for so much humanity, I thought, but graciously accepted. It never occurred to me who my companion would be until a knock roused me from my undressing.

A lady, bagged, long-booted, long-coated, and spurred, presented herself. This isn't possible! It cannot be. Really.

My reactions were surprise—amazement—astonishment.

The attendant put it right. A gallant Commander gave up his single berth for my society and, I must add, to enable the Bagged-Booted one to have a room of her own for the journey.

How different Laurence Sterne?

He would have closed with the adventure. I am a poor fish. I contented myself with my gallant Commander's company and slept, undisturbed, all the way to Drem.

HOTEL IN EDINBURGH — Wednesday

THE hub of Edinburgh is what they call "The Mound"—an open space in the centre of Princes Street which divides East Princes Street Gardens from West Princes Street Gardens and from which arises a winding road which takes the foot passengers and the tramway up past the Bank of Scotland, past the Sheriff Court House—the road skirts the City Hall or Chambers, as they call it—opposite is St. Giles Cathedral, and it leads on to the Police Offices and the old Houses of Parliament and so to the Old Town.

In the centre of The Mound are the Royal Academy and the National Gallery, two buildings similar in style, one holding the art of the past and the other the art of to-day and to-morrow.

At eleven this morning I was fortunate; the London train had miscarried—something had happened and the Minister was unable to keep his appointment. My elaborate preparations, files, forms, and memoranda were, at any rate temporarily, of no moment and, pending information as to what was to happen, I felt myself free for the forenoon. At eleven I was at The Mound and learned that the Director of the National Gallery had provided facilities for an exhibition. We have seen all sorts of exhibitions here, if not from China to Peru at least from China to Canada, and I went in to hear what was being said about this latest display. Sir Malcolm Robertson was the principal speaker, the chairman of the British Council, a finished, polished, bland, distinguished, presentable speaker indeed he is. He had, of course, as a support, that ubiquitous pair in this city, Lord Rosebery and the Lord Provost, and with him the Minister whose country was responsible for the exhibition. Sir Malcolm speaks well. He presents the British Council adequately and I feel I want to commend the British Council to myself, in spite of a certain reluctance. Being a good Englishman, I imagine the habit of self-advertisement is not natural to me. We should not advertise. The English are not blatant. The Germans say "Deutschland über Alles," but we only pray that God will save our King.

I think it is a little overdone. We, as a nation, should present ourselves, first of all to ourselves and later to the world at large. The British Council is justified in that it makes an organized and serious attempt when opportunity occurs, to carry out these essential duties. We are a great people and, while modesty is a private virtue, I am not sure that it is one which goes well with public affairs. And yet this exhibition, for all its admirable presentation, is too modest. War time may make the collection and arrangement a special problem no doubt, but when present-time restrictions are removed, it is hoped there will be no inhibitions preventing us from declaring to a world, not fully recognizing our greatness, our contribution to the welfare of mankind.

"What do they know of England who only England know?" is a challenge to us and to others. We want to build upon a proven greatness. It is no accident that we stood alone when the highly civilized peoples like the Danes and the Norwegians and the Dutch surrendered, when the barbarian peoples like the Russians temporized with a situation with which they felt they were not nearly ready to deal . . . we are right to assert that, although we were not ready, we were not unwilling to accept world leadership with all the painful consequences that it involved. This story should be told, told by poet and painter, dramatized, told by artist and by actor, should be told all the world over, and for that reason I hope that young Mr. Harvey Wood—who most obligingly talked to me after the exhibition had been opened—I hope that young Mr. Harvey Wood and many like him will come forward increasingly in the days that are to be, telling the world our story, making us proud that we are part of it, inspiring us to live not only up to the glories of our past but to the limitless future which awaits those who are not afraid, with sharpened swords, to seek the glittering prizes.

EDINBURGH Thursday

WITH a glass of very expensive but excellent whisky before

me, I am responsive to the cry for justice by the distillers of Scotland. Here they have a pleasant rural industry based upon barley. Here they have a unique process whereby they produce an acceptable and wholesome beverage. Here they have a world-wide demand. Here they have something which carries the name of Scotland far and wide. Here they have something that poets have praised and careworn men consumed.

And here we have something which is the subject of penal taxation to the detriment of Scotland's industry. It is the major injustice which Scotland endures. Why not tax cotton as you tax whisky?

Ask Lancashire what she thinks of that?

The Scotch are extraordinarily supine about this matter and I cannot tell why. Is it patriotism? Do they feel that no price is too high to pay for freedom and that they should pay it in the way that hurts them most? A tax on their porridge would be too light an enactment, leaving them almost unscathed, except in purse.

Perhaps.

There is another reason given, and this by a minister—a clergyman—whisky is sin. Scotchmen were told by Mr. John Calvin of Geneva, where they make gin, I am told, that they were original sinners. A Scotchman always pays his way—even reluctantly. He endures the high cost of original sin and pays, patriotically, its price.

EDINBURGH Friday

"SHE walks the lady of my delight, a shepherdess of sheep. . . ." "She walks" are the operative words. How well these Scotch girls walk, or is it Princes Street that gives them a setting?

Piccadilly and Princes Street—streets with shops and houses on one side and gardens on the other, these are proper—well—is proper the word exactly?—these are attractive places for my lady as she walks abroad.

Princesses, one might say, in Princes Street and Piccadilly. How well these Scotch girls carry themselves, was my reflection. They have reddish faces, uncultivated complexions in the main, coats unbuttoned, swinging and showing a dress and underneath—bare—and again, reddish legs—stout, clattering shoes, for many I observe have taken to the wooden sabot kind of shoes—there they are: Scotch lassies as they call them, in Princes Street in war time, all in the morning early.

They are clerks and shopworkers. The industrial sort affect the blue overall trousered suits and rakish, practical hats and scarves, but there are fewer of them. Those who are about at nine in the morning are special shoppers, chasing a bargain in between shifts, I conclude.

Writers even of such obscure books as diaries do not describe often enough the ordinary surroundings of our lives. We take our environment for granted. We do not detail it or analyse it. We see it but we do not observe it. I must practise observation more.

Yesterday at the new munition works I jostled elbow to elbow Sir Stafford Cripps, the Minister of Aircraft Production. I might have jostled him in Delhi or in Moscow, but it was in Edinburgh this time that I met this most travelled Minister of the Crown.

And what do I remember about him? What did I observe? Let me see what floats still unsunk on the surface of recollection. His wife was with him. She looked pleasant. He wore—what did he wear? He said—what did he say—Oh! yes—location of industry—diversification of employment—and for the rest there remains an impression of ascetic purpose, high concentration, determination. He is a restless—perhaps a resistless—force. He energizes. He drives himself, albeit on a diet of herbs, for he eats no meat. Whither will he go? I venture to prophesy he will go far.

AT HOME Saturday

SAMUEL PEPYS wrote over a million words, wrote himself blind, in fact, but wrote himself immortal.

Diary keeping is not the most often chosen road to fame, in fact few have found it—none, I doubt, have dreamed their diary keeping was destined to make them famous.

The diary, pure and simple, is severely limited. The events of the day are poor things for others, rich only because they are our own. George Grossmith's "Diary of a Nobody" owes its interest to this quality. It emphasizes pathetically the long littleness of life. Pepys is the best of the real diarists. Evelyn, whose record runs for seventy years, comes next. The journal diary offers more scope and, if Pepys leads in one field, surely Boswell leads in the other. Wesley, Haydon, Walter Scott, Creevey, Emerson . . . I have them all and I am grateful for the introduction they give me into the minds of some interesting and several really great men.

My own day has given me as good as—even better than, I think—some of those of yesterday.

"Private Papers of Henry Ryecroft," George Gissing's best writing, is one. J. A. Spender's "Comments of Bagshot" is another. Barbellion's "Journal of a Disappointed Man" is a third, and there are Katherine Mansfield and George Sturt, all as well worth meeting as Wesley or Emerson or even he whom the Scotch call "the Great Sir Walter." I read them all when I am at home, but I carry none with me on my journeyings. Sufficient unto the day are my own diaries and my own journal can contain all my journeyings in body and in spirit.

It is good to be a civil servant. I like its circumscription. I like my limited responsibility—my "red tape-ry"—my Minister—my orders—my restrictions. Who would be free? Who would be an individualist?

So I think, but it is a passing thought.

So I think to-day which is Saturday, but the night cometh and there too is Monday when I go to King's Cross on my way to God knows what crosses awaiting me at the station of the cross, at the Waverley, Edinburgh.

EDINBURGH Tuesday

THERE is nothing but trouble. That man is born to it is no solace. It is irksome, irritating, intolerable, whether it be a hole in one's sock or the unexpected toothache or the sufferings of a dear friend. But what are the alternatives?

Ease, comfort, effortless success, facile attainment; the human spirit finds no satisfaction, no comfort in these.

Man is at his best as he fronts the Hill of Difficulty or stumbles in the Valley of the Shadow.

Man is at his noblest when hemmed about by his enemies. His fair-weather friends desert him and he sees that his most faithful, devoted, good companions are pain, trial, trouble.

They do not desert him, indeed, lo! they are with him always, even unto the end of the world.

Equip thy soul for the battle, is good counsel for the man who knows for what he is born inevitably. Who reads William James these days, I wonder? An hour too early for the train at King's Cross, I went into the British Museum and read in his "Principles of Psychology." I copied this—it served me well all the week:

"Every day deny thyself some satisfaction: thine eyes—mere curiosity: thy tongue—everything that may hold vanity or vent enmity: thy palate—dainties: (ah! how useful that was to me in the Hotel at York) thy ears—flattery: thy body—ease and luxury."

Yes, there is nothing but trouble. My sleeper was taken by the Ministry of Information.

HOTEL, EDINBURGH Wednesday

I REFLECT she does it divinely. It is just as much an art being a duchess as being a designer or a dishwasher. Daring to be a duchess, these days, requires as much courage as daring to be a Daniel in the days of Nebuchadnezzar.

She opened a bazaar—a collection of mostly unwanted, useless, ugly things which had this in common that the donors with one mind were prepared to part with them at any price—for the Red Cross. Putting her bag and her long gloves down on the Union Jack covered table, the duchess confessed the pleasure it gave her to be here, her appreciation of the work of the Red Cross, her personal knowledge of the excellent work it did, her hopes that the bazaar would be a great success, "and so I declare it open."

Everybody cheered. Everybody was glad. Everybody felt it was all right.

The duchess said to the chairwoman, "Did I do all right?"

The chairwoman beamed happily and a plain woman rose to move a vote of thanks. The duchess responded. I paid half a crown for a cup of tea but, as I walked back to the office, I felt I had my money's worth.

I am inconsistently all for democracy and, at the same time, all for duchesses. What use is a democracy to me if it has no duchesses? I want a rich, romantic, colourful life for the people and they can't have it without Duchesses.

Democracy without Duchesses is like gin without Italian, soup without salt, pictures without frames—nay, more, love without kisses.

HOTEL, GLASGOW Friday

AMONG all the plans of the planners I have not yet found one which, once the war is over, seems to me to be as urgent and as desirable as my own.

Let us have a plan for tidying up the place! These odd corners, these bits of waste land, these crude heaps of tin-cans and ashes, these coal bings, these decayed buildings of brick and wood and corrugated iron; let us plan to do away with them.

This is a little island. There is no room for untidiness and disorder. If a bit of land can't be cultivated or used as a site for a building of some sort, make a beauty spot of it—a place with seats and shrubs—or any way clear it up and let it cease to be an eyesore.

Every municipality, every village, should have as one of its slogans "Away with eyesores."

The bings, a civil engineer told me to-day as we passed through Lanarkshire, need not be. There should be a survey made of these excrescences and depressions. The depressions are often useless, untidy ditches which would become good, useful land if scientifically filled up with the bing refuse and adequately top-dressed. Others could be planted. There are shrubs which will grow on them.

And in the future bing refuse should be left below or, if brought to the surface, replaced. All things are bought with a price and beauty, in England, green and pleasant, must be paid for. It will be worth the money.

HOME Sunday

In the year 1928, writing on Monday, 31st December, in his journal, Arnold Bennett states he wrote 304,000 words. He deducted from the year a full month given to rehearsals and six weeks to holidays. It is a splendid achievement for one who not only wrote but wrote well.

There is, Newman Flower told me, a falling off in the demand for Arnold Bennett. It is a poorer world which does not know him. I put him, in sheer human interest, above Wells and Shaw and Galsworthy. He inspires me.

The consciousness of defects of education and experience, his faithful practice of his craft, his natural and his assumed, vanities; these make him for me a likeable, a lovable figure.

Once I projected an anthology to be entitled "The Best of Bennett," but publishers were not encouraging and he was too good, I concluded, for his best to be printed in one volume.

He will come again.

Everlasting life for an author is a thin immortality, a ghostly business, a thin paper edition.

Arnold Bennett has a greater, braver fate awaiting him.

I prophesy a glorious resurrection when he will be acclaimed by a new generation of the lovers of literature.

They will rediscover him as they are rediscovering Anthony Trollope, and in their rediscovery they will discover our generation—the nineteens, 1914-1918—the years between. I am glad in a way Arnold Bennett did not see 1939. He saw the best of his generation; he had "a good time."

HOTEL, EDINBURGH Tuesday

SHALL I give up? The question is posed by a very successful man of affairs. He is sixty odd. If he were in the Civil Service he could go at sixty with a K.C.B. and a modified pension, or stick it out to sixty-five—perhaps a K.B.E. or nothing at all—and a full pension. How well the Civil Service is arranged, or how well it manages itself! My business friend is free: he is master of his destiny. What a tragedy!

Who wants to be master of his destiny at sixty? Are there not hot bottles in bed on a cold night—anxious mornings, when to read the paper in bed until ten is the antechamber to paradise—what is there in business to equal these attractions? Frankly, I don't think there is anything, but I am biased. I am a public employee! I am glad I am only temporarily so employed. I do not love the State. Like Walter Raleigh, I sometimes think

> "I do not love the Human Race,
> I do not like its silly face."

But I am not myself to-night. The committee lasted from 2.30 p.m. till well after 6 p.m.

Need human affairs be so complicated? Must so few make so much trouble for so many? Must I keep going on? Am I not entitled to realize the dream of years gone by? What was it again?

> "From birth to five—first stage—
> Five to fifteen—boyhood—
> Fifteen to twenty-one—adolescence—
> Next thirty years—to work—
> Then choice, freedom, leisure, roses, books, travel."

That was it.

It seems very remote to-night.

EDINBURGH Wednesday

"THERE is a man steeped in crime!" So said a dark complexioned bookseller to me as I was looking over a shelf of books in a bookshop to-day. I turned my head slightly, I did not like to appear curious, and among four men who stood nearby—one had his back to me—I could see none who seemed to answer the description. "A man steeped in crime" seems a simple enough phrase, but what does such a man look like? Are his cuffs bloodstained? Does his pocket bulge with pistols? Does his waistbelt hold a knife? Does his face emphasize his villainy? I don't know. I said "Where? Who? Who is he?" and quietly and gently the bookseller said to me "It is William Roughead."

William Roughead, of course, is a man steeped in crime. Is he not one of the begetters of the "Notable Trials" books? I had not expected he would look like he does. What preconceived ideas I had of a man steeped in crime I don't know, but William Roughead seemed bland, genial, with a round, reddish, humorous Scotch face and twinkling eyes. He seemed a quizzical, jolly-looking man. He was talking to one of the other booksellers, talking in a lively way, and both seemed to be enjoying the conversation.

What takes a man to crime? A reference to the courts will show . . . greed, envy, evil intentions, hate . . . heaven knows the category is a long one, but what takes a respectable, humane, distinguished lawyer into a study of crime is another story. I cannot tell, but what I can tell is what William Roughead writes always finds a very considerable public. Crime seems fascinating to those who live crimeless lives, those whose days are spent in innocent endeavour.

There is an explanation, I have no doubt, why calm, cool, collected Civil Servants turn to crime as a contrast to the blameless simplicity and innocence of their lives, and this bland gentleman steeps himself in crime in order that they may have their blood bath.

It is life's fallacious, unsatisfactory reasoning. Sometimes I cannot explain myself, not even in the pages of this blameless diary.

LONDON Friday

SOME days the day will not start. I have lost the key to open the door, I don't know the switch wherewith to start the works, the whole creation groaneth and travaileth . . .

some days it is rather unaccountable . . . one does not know why everything just goes crosswise.

To-day, of course, I have no such excuse. Things didn't go well this morning because they went too merrily last night. Like Shakespeare's Cassio, I come to the view that at my time of life I have poor, unhappy brains for drinking, a little now goes a long way. A little is sometimes necessary to clear the dullness of my mind, to brighten the immediate present, to tinge with some little hope the far horizons, a little—but a little only.

Age is an easily reached milestone.

There has not been the same agitation this war as last for national prohibition. Have we learned a lesson about it? I would like to see the qualities heightened. Some of the things that pass as British wines and English vermouth are offences against the body politic and the stomach. Ordinarily, they would not be allowed, but how we are to prevent them I don't know. Price does not seem to matter. You cannot tell how bad they are until you have taken them.

There is only one safety and security and that is in self-denial, and I look forward to the day when wine will be wine again and all the other good gifts of nature, especially the Scotch ones, will be reliable, available at reasonable prices and in suitable quantities for those who must necessarily take something, not only for their health's sake but to relieve the plain, unbearable, unendurable ache of merely living. How many teetotalers are there in public affairs? How many positive teetotalers get things done? Are there any, anyway? Is strong drink a necessity for the western civilization?

"Here lies one whose name was writ in water"—that was John Keats's epitaph, but who else is there in the glowing paths of history of whom the same thing can be said?

AT HOME IN SURREY Saturday

In spite of the disturbances which come to the south-west of London, I always return to it with a good deal of satisfaction. The cool, classic serenity of the City of Edinburgh is all very well, but there is something very pleasant about Surrey. The housekeeper welcomes me. The ageing gardener, having told me of his son-in-law's achievement in the Airborne Division, condescends to offer me the lettuce and the cabbage, and these, for my palate, are different from and better than all the productions of the market gardens around Edinburgh.

The housekeeper and the gardener told me that St. Martha's are having their bazaar and that it has been arranged for me to open it.

They see so little of me, they think I would be an attraction—more so, perhaps, than some remote notability. My absence has made the heart of my fellow-parishioners grow fonder, and I was begged to open the bazaar.

It is a considerable picture. Standing on a platform in an English church hall, looking at the faces of the simple folk crowded at an unaccustomed hour on a Saturday morning in a plain, utilitarian building, a building devoted to choir practise and Sunday School, to Bible class and work party; I will look down on that as the Vicar gives me a word of welcome—how much they value my association with them—how they hope I will be safeguarded on my travels (how incredible; they think to be in Scotland is to be in greater danger than in London)—they have appreciated my very generous gifts to the vegetable stall and how they welcome me here this morning to declare the Sale of Work and Bazaar open.

On my feet, I will stammer some words—how I appreciate their kindness—Scotland is all right but there is no place like home—I hope the sale will be a success—we want to send any comfort we can to the fighting men and women . . . how wonderful they are, pretending so seriously and so successfully to carry on in their English way with their anxieties and fears and worries uncountable, presenting themselves on this occasion full of good intentions and good works. I will sit down and they will move a vote of thanks to me; all too generous, and the platform party will stumble down the four steps to the floor. Round the stalls I will go. What a pathetic collection will be presented —vases and Benares ware, pots and pans, pieces of embroidery proudly ticketed "without coupons" and equally gallantly sold at prices which seem already to recognize that the American estimate of the value of the £ is universally accepted. I will buy, probably—a piece of old English china—a crude model of the Prince of Wales, or Queen Victoria as a girl—they always have them. One would not believe the human mind could conceive such monstrosities, much less produce them, but produced they were, I think originally in Birmingham in the 1850's.

What a romance life is—far away, Princes Street, Edinburgh—remote seems my bed in the Station Hotel, lonely and deserted the Ministry, idle and apart lies my leather case with my initials stamped in gold thereon; I am here with the English, especially the Englishwomen, quiet and proud and happy to accept a welcome from fellow-parishioners; back it seems to me, for a few hours in safety in his own home, to his own housekeeper and gardener, safe and well from the remote, terrible dangers of Scotland!

LODGINGS, EDINBURGH Monday

THIS house was built about 1815. Its first tenants were émigrés. The French Revolution was over, and these French folk had said goodbye to the France they knew.

I wonder how I would do as a refugee. Could I settle down—find a new way of life—make a livelihood? I admire the way some have been able to do it, especially the Channel Islanders. I saw some of them up here on the west coast of Scotland, determined philosophically to make the most and the best of it. There is a daily bravery which out-faces the sudden courage of the soldier who rushes the machine gun post or the airman who, broken and burning alive, stands to his ship and his duty. Oldish folk—uprooted—ruined—it is no less a sublime courage that they show as they take up broken life anew.

This war has brought much humiliation. Burma, Malaya, China—these can be borne perhaps, but the Channel Islands—we bear the loss of them too lightly. An Islander said to me, "You hold Malta but not Jersey, the Faroes, and the Orkneys, but not Alderney and Sark." I have no answer. It is not my department.

"You must ask my right honourable friend, the Prime Minister." I avow he feels it. He has an historical sense. They came to us when the Normans came to England. They have been independent, they have been part of France, they have been part of England. Now, for the first time, they are held by Germany.

I don't like it.

Nobody can like it.

EDINBURGH Tuesday

ARNOLD BENNETT found it necessary to have a technique in

his search for lively ideas. He used to go and sit in the National Gallery in Trafalgar Square or the Express Dairy tea shop in Chelsea, and ideas just flowed, if he was lucky.

I find the telephone directory best for me, especially the two volume London one.

The Scotch ones are not so good although of them the Glasgow one is the best. Whats-his-name—the county-clerk—tells me he refreshes his mind with Whitaker's Almanack, especially the index. I tried it. It doesn't work with me, but I have observed that there are over 100 pages in that work given over to the addresses of Government offices. That is a lively thought. Cecil Palmer, the anti-servile state perfervid Individualist, tells me that a dozen years ago there was only a page or so in Whitaker for this purpose. I believe him.

"Power corrupts and absolute power corrupts absolutely." The State grows on what it feeds on, and it feeds on power. My colleagues in the higher Civil Service agree for the most part. Every Department is overgrown except their own, and there are special reasons for that.

We should stop it. Where is Canute or Mrs. Partington to stop the rising tides of bureaucracy? I look hopefully—Mrs. Partington—to the Throne of the Kitchen. There is little hope elsewhere.

EDINBURGH Wednesday

THEY hold the view that a man may be a pacifist and yet logically and conscientiously be a Civil Servant. You may serve the State but take no part in its defence. You may be its clerk but not its soldier. It defeats me. I admit a mental incapacity—and I am not one to rate consistency or logic highly in human values.

It was ever thus: we are, in its most discreditable sense, a peace-loving country.

The fighting men have their place in our ballads, in our songs, in our charitable lists, and in our Public Assistance registers. They have little place elsewhere—it is a fault in our countrymen; we ignored the passionate pleadings of Lord Roberts in his day, we were deaf, contemptuously deaf, to Mr. Winston Churchill in our own day.

Will it always be so—this toleration of the illogical, the unpatriotic, the craven?

For England's sake it is to be hoped that the answer is no! And so I unburden myself, but it is of no avail. It will always be so. The thing that is, is the thing that shall be.

It is comforting to know that we cannot dodge destiny. I remind myself of Henry who didn't go to the last war as he ought and who was killed, rather painfully, in a motor accident—in a motor he had bought with his war profits.

We cannot avoid the inevitable.

Fate—nay God—is not mocked. He balances His ledgers.

How often I think that!

HOME Sunday

We are a great people, and, fortunately, our best native productions are not for export.

I write "fortunately" because I think that no country in the world would take Herbert Morrison, the Minister of Home Security.

He is a British product—an English product—a Cockney product, and he is London's Own.

I place him as the first of politicians. He knows politics, plays the game of politics with knowledge and interest and, indeed, with passion.

I like him for it, too.

He knows men and women, rates them not too high but, better still, rates them not too low. With good fortune he will lead the Left. He won't be happy always with them but he will serve this day and generation of his countrymen.

He has a sense of order. His father was a policeman; he understands law as well as order, and he knows that they are essential. His passionate love for London is almost moving. He talked about some name for the Leader of London. I would call him Chancellor of the County of London—Lord Chancellor might be better.

We dearly love a lord, we English.

We would more dearly love a Lord Chancellor of London, we Londoners!

Chairman of the London County Council is a poor title.

London ought to have something better. I must send him the suggestion.

HOTEL, KING'S CROSS — Monday

"A TRAVELLER in Little Things" is the title of one of W. H. Hudson's books.

I sometimes feel I am that. In my satchel are my papers: memoranda, two Stationery Office prints, a flat box of cigarettes and the usual mass of notes and addresses, interviews, and other scrap.

I wish I had some more elation to bring to my task. I am just sent hither and thither from Waverley to King's Cross—from King's Cross to Waverley. "Going by Railroad," wrote John Ruskin in "Modern Painters," "I do not consider travelling at all. It is merely being sent to a place and very little different from becoming a parcel." Frankly, Mr. Ruskin, being a parcel is better. You are handled with care, you are insulated with corrugated paper and bound up with twine.

While I bump my way along the platform, I envy the parcels. They are neatly stacked on an electric trolley and a lady (who was once a barmaid, she told me) in trousers has them propelled along. There is room for them in the van—there is room for all the parcels that come.

How are the mighty fallen! How easily blazing ambition is snuffed out! I am ashamed of myself, I who aspired to a C.B.E. am now fallen so low that I envy a parcel.

I am a traveller in little things, very small beer, I fear, in a very small parcel.

Or is it a cracked bottle?

HOTEL, EDINBURGH Tuesday

To-day I escaped. It is a good plan to escape. "No," I told my secretary, "I have an engagement all that afternoon." That was days ago and she had barraged all attempts to encroach on me. Poor thing. She doesn't know. At 5 when I returned she doesn't know. I only hope no one has seen me.

Here am I, a distinguished—albeit, temporary public servant, taking the afternoon off to go to the pictures! And in a week-day too! And at a crisis—there is always a crisis—in the nation's affairs! Who would have believed it? I will tell you. Samuel Pepys, he would have believed it. Francis Drake, he would have believed it, and behind two such stout Englishmen who knew wars and crises I shelter myself. I confess to these pages I lunched on lobster and half a bottle of hock (how rare hock is—how rarer it will be!) and went to see the new film "The Life and Death of Colonel Blimp."

Low, licensed by the *Evening Standard,* mocked at the Old Glory, the Old Boy, the Old School Tie, Bangalore and Bloemfontein, Ypres, and the Somme, and all that, and he got his reward—paid in cash, signed, sealed and delivered. But the counter-attack! Mr. Low didn't count on the counter-attack. The Tories have triumphed; I mean those Tories who know that two parts of his-tory are Tory—the last two—the final syllables. We win the last battle. We utter the last or the two last—syllables. Colonel Blimp, the figure of fun in the film, as in life, wins—wins on merit, wins on pathos, wins on achievement, wins on humanity. Colonel Blimp, if his reception this afternoon is a criterion, has triumphed, and David Low is only as he wants to be—Low.

OFFICE, EDINBURGH Thursday

THERE are moments when the best in us makes the worst of us. The world is too much with me in this City of Seven Hills, this Northern Temple of the Winds, this Athens of the North.

Walking along the street in profound depression, engendered, I am convinced, by eating fish meal fed bacon, a lady bowed to me.

Life looked up. The sun of my soul shone.

She was in the earliest thirties, a lovely time for a woman, and wore a hat with violets on it—nodding violets—a saucy hat. She was dark and had dancing eyes, and she smiled as she bowed her head.

"Good Morning," she said.

It is enough. I don't know her—but it is enough. The dayspring from on high has visited me. The rainbow is in the sky. Life is filled with promise again and I have lost the profound depression engendered by eating fish meal fed bacon. The Gadarene swine have run down a steep place and are lost for ever in the bottomless depression of the salt estranging sea.

I go on my way rejoicing. Nothing that the Minister of Information on whom I attend to-day may say can discourage me. I am armoured against everything. I am bright, burnished, breezy, brotherly. The fish meal fed bacon has departed. The glory has dawned.

But now I am discouraged again. What I have written is a piece of recollection. Leigh Hunt has done it better. I remember.

"Jenny kissed me when we met,
Jumping from the chair she sat in;
Time, you thief, you love to get
Sweets into your list—put that in;
Say I'm weary, say I'm sad,
Say that health and wealth have missed me,
Say I'm growing old, but add
Jenny kissed me."

It is misquoted, I fear—but anyway my Jill with the hat is as good as Leigh Hunt's Jenny.

HOME Sunday

In the days of my youth I was inclined to think of myself as a sceptic. I was the doubting Thomas in my little society. Belief, faith, these things made me scoff; a planned universe, a socialist state, a land flowing with milk and honey . . . I could not bring myself to believe that such things could be.

Once—as for Heaven and Hell and the Goodness of God and the Babe of Bethlehem—these were absurdities—fictions—fancies—not worth discussing.

Now I think I am wiser. I certainly am older and I don't doubt anything now. Trust is the keynote of my outlook nowadays; give him a chance, is often in my thoughts and sometimes in my acts.

It is better so. It is better than doubt and dismal fears for the worst. It used to be too good to be true. Now nothing is too good to be true. I feel I can believe anything is possible.

That is personal progress, I claim. God looked on the world and found it was good. We ought all, if we live faithfully and fortunately, to come to that conclusion. The dark destiny of man is not proven. The miracle of being born is not the only miracle, I am convinced. Why should it be? Why shouldn't life be roomy yet? Someone has written:

> "Mineral died and there was plant.
> Plant died and there is animal.
> Animal died and there is man.
> What is less by dying?"

Who was it? I forget.

I have an untidy memory but one day I will know all even as I am known.

HOME Tuesday

YOUNG CHARLEY'S death, after weeks of "missing over Berlin," has hit me. My faith in the life to come is shaken. Does God balance His accounts in the end, justly? I have always believed it. I still hold to it.

To-day I have been to the cemetery. How unworthy are these city cemeteries of ours! Acres of turf and gravelled walks covered with up-ended stones and pillars and slabs. Can we not do better? We can. My father and mother and uncle and sister lie in their resting graves; a stone tells their birth day and their death day and on the pediment I read "For ever with the Lord."

I am the lawful owner of the plot of ground. I would willingly give up my title if all head stones were removed.

You would then have a God's Acre of green turf, continuous, unbroken by wallflowers and glass wreaths and bulbs. If remembrance required a stimulus—on the surrounding walls the names of those buried might be recorded on a mural tablet. For the rest, nothing but the carpet of green turf, a haunt of ancient peace.

The monumental masons wouldn't like it; the importers of Carrara marble and the granite merchants of Aberdeen would have to console the manufacturers of artificial wreaths with glass cases, but cities and towns would have seemlier places in which to bury their dead or scatter the ashes. It is one of the things I will take up if I ever become a City Councillor.

Ah! There is a far horizon—there is a new world to conquer. It has its attractions, undoubted attractions, but I must go to bed.

The earliest train for Edinburgh is my first objective to-morrow.

HOTEL, EDINBURGH Wednesday

JAMES ELROY FLECKER always has an appeal for me. It may be because I saw his play "Hassan" in His Majesty's Theatre in 1924 with, who was she?—I forget—or because of his lovely poetry and his death at Davos in 1915 when he was only thirty.

I think it is the poetry and the lines he wrote "To a poet a thousand years hence." These are the lines for the diarist who dreams as Pepys never did of a future he will never see with mortal eye.

> "I who am dead a thousand years
> And wrote this sweet archaic song,
> Send you my words for messengers
> The way I shall not pass along."

Lots of us should be doing diaries. There will be curiosity about our lives. They will want to know how we lived in our finest hour. They will want to know how we did and did without, and what we wore.

I like to think so, but as I write I am chilled with doubt. Other lines come to my mind. I can't remember who wrote them.

> "Why should I fret unwilling ears
> With old songs sung anew."

No reason. There is no reason at all. I will put this book of writing away. I will pack my bag for to-morrow. I have a routine—my spare shirt and two collars—they go in to-night, but my pyjamas, dressing wrap and shaving things they go in to-morrow morning with these writing things. I am a methodical man. A reliable though temporary civil servant, I live from day to day and my secret, nay, open vice is that I am an incorrigible diarist.

CLYDESIDE Thursday

ONCE—this year—I had a conversation with Hatteras about the best line in English prose, but it didn't come to much. It was a miserable day and we met in one of these terrible war-time canteens. I have been jotting down in my Charles Letts' pocket-book diary, however. They make good reading on a railway journey. Take out the pocket-book, read the line, close the eyes—it is an infallible remedy for train travel boredom.

To-day I have added one of the best and very little known as far as I can discover.

Sir William Napier was Wellington's historian. He asserts of the Peninsular War that he was either an eye witness or got his facts from Persons (the capital is his) of no mean authority, and I get my line from his short history, "English Battles and Sieges in the Peninsula." He is relating the Assault of Badajos in April, 1812. He tells of the storming of the Castle and the death of Colonel Ridge. "The enemy," he relates, "retired; but Ridge fell, and no man died that night with more glory—yet many died, and there was much glory." Not just heroism, he seems to say, but heroism built on heroism, heroism on a background entirely heroic.

They don't write like that to-day. I would be heartened if they did, and yet heroism as lofty is the daily tale of the sea and the air, and may well be if my experience last war is a guide, a daily tale on land.

I wish I could have got into the army, I reflect, but it is a passing thought. It is wishful thinking and, as such, High Treason to the Department.

HOTEL, EDINBURGH Friday

THIS Savings Movement is the successor of the Women's Freedom Movement of the last war. They had to find something for the women to do. The ordinary woman who has her home to attend to and her daily work to discharge, she has to have occupation and not mere occupation, but useful worth-while occupation. Last war, of course, we saw Mrs. Pankhurst and the Women's Social and Political Union . . . "we must have the vote" and "why doesn't the Government allow woman to take her place and share in public affairs." These are over in this war.

Women have scores of opportunities—the Women's Voluntary Service, nursing, munitions. In St. Andrew's House there must be a thousand of them. The unwanted woman does not exist. She is the fair quarry of the Minister of Labour and he pursues her relentlessly.

The big thing they have done, and I don't think it has been appreciated at its proper level, is the organization of street savings and door to door collections. Edinburgh has led this country in that kind of work. I must note the galaxy of remarkable women whose names I will want to remember when I come to re-read this diary. . . .

Mrs. Tod with a husband in North Africa; Mrs. West Russell with a husband who was with the Canadians; Mrs. George Hay whose husband is an Alderman—I ought to say a "Bailie"—of the city.

These three I will always remember as typical of this movement into which they put the energy and vigour that their mothers might have put into the demand for the vote. They have organized demonstrations and they have great men to come and speak to them. Last year it was Kingsley

Wood, the Fighting Chancellor if ever there was one, and he delivered himself of an oration to a large assembly. The next year they matched that by demanding the services of the Minister of Food. He has the advantage, of course, of being familiar with what women want. I know that he was in big business, running shops for the people in Lancashire and elsewhere before he took up public office. He looks all right too. I can quite understand the ladies loving him. One I heard referred to him and said she knew him. She called him Fred Marquis and said he should have retained that name—he was wrong to take the name of Lord Woolton, he would have been better as Lord Marquis! That makes me chuckle. I wonder if he thought of it. A Peer is all right, but to be a Lord Marquis very nearly reaches the level of My Lord Duke.

My pen runs on. In half an hour I will be in the train. This diary I will lock in my satchel and impressively proceed to the lift, descend to the railway platform, say "Good Evening" to Mr. Craig, the Station-master of the Waverley, and ensconce myself in my berth. I will not forget the women at whose Rally I have been privileged to attend to-night. But one is safer to go to bed without the women. It is a narrow bed in which one is not only possessed of a single thought but of a single mind.

Fortunate Sir Kingsley Wood and Lord Woolton that they can command the plaudits of the people. I sometimes wish I were a politician.

HOTEL, EDINBURGH Sunday

It was great good fortune for a diarist to meet Montgomery —Lieutenant General Sir Bernard Montgomery, C.B., D.S.O., to be more—if not entirely—exact.

He had never been in Edinburgh and the King told him to go there and make the Lord Provost show him his city—so I was informed. Anyway, there he was all in the morning early at the Waverley Station. My contact was slight enough but I must record it—as Samuel Pepys would have done. (I remember Pepys travelling too—his "step down" to Portsmouth—reporting and conferring with Sir Richard Beach, the President Commission, and, then to the King at Windsor, first thing next morning.)

He was received on the platform by the Lord Provost majestically making an elaborate salute and there were other soldiers there too. General Sir Andrew Thorne, Commander-in-Chief of all Scotland. They talked for a moment or two together—they went into the train in which Montgomery had travelled—I hovered, wavered, hesitated, moved away from the Military Police, and then drew nearer and caught sight of these highly coloured personages signing the General's book. And then they whirled away and for me they were lost.

Assiduous snatcher-up of trifles, collector of gossip, pryer into personalia that I am, I learned in the hotel in the afternoon all that had happened and where they had been. The Great Montgomery went around the town with the Lord Provost—and heaven knows what conversations took place between them . . . neither of them is lacking in speech nor, externally at any rate, a bashful man. They went to the Saint Giles Church together and were photographed and by one, precisely, the General was in his train again and on his way to inspect, I conclude although I am not allowed to say, his invasion troops.

In the hotel, Auld said Montgomery was not as wonderful as we think.

Simms of the Ministry of War Transport reminded us that Napoleon favoured lucky generals.

I am like Napoleon, and I wish Montgomery, if he has ever had it, more and more and more luck.

EDINBURGH Monday

"CRUELTY—that I cannot bear—it is so wanton—so unnecessary—so futile."

It was a crisis—a culmination—a fitting ending to desultory talk which began at King's Cross and now was passing Berwick.

The Jews—how cruel the Nazis were to them—foxes—the hunting of them—how civilized beings who thought themselves ladies and gentlemen—how could they do it—and performing animals—it was done with heated irons—and the navy too—they weren't entirely free of blame—millions of wild sea birds are caught and drowned in oceans of thick black oil—but the navy were not alone—the army had courts martial (she was very accurate about this "courts martial"—not " court martials") and there was practically, I mean *practically* the third degree—AND the police—you know about the conscientious objectors—not that I agree with them but they have their civil rights—I positively KNOW . . . cruelty everywhere. The train thundered along. We were at Drem. As we started again—the Hater of Cruelty had left at Drem—a handsome stout lady of sixty in mourning who had hardly spoken at all, leaned over me.

I thought she was going to tell me of some cruel bereavement. I braced myself. I reflected we would soon be at the Waverley.

"The cruellest thing I know is the way in which some women can eat what they like and still have figures like forks!"

"Storks, did you say?" "No, not STORKS—FORKS! It is a crying shame. I know no cruelty like it."

I dared say nothing. I helped her down with her bags. I was glad it was Waverley.

EDINBURGH, AT A CONFERENCE OF THE MINISTRY OF SUPPLY — Tuesday

TUESDAY is not my favourite day, but it is a favourite day with those who desire to confer. There is Sunday for prayers and Monday to see that they are faithfully fulfilled, but by Tuesday the papers are ready and chairs are set, blotting paper is on the table, the carafe with the utility tumbler duly cleaned, and all is ready . . . the chairman begins. This considerable ritual is the ritual of the English. They take memoranda papers, planning papers, references and cross references, and from this jungle of activity there emerges the conference. Any subject will do but it happens to be a new kind of house. Its name is an inspiration. I am often struck by the appositeness of names. If there is a gateway to the New Jerusalem, what more suitable than to discover that it is a Portal?

The Portal House is the application of mass production to mass demand. It seems to have been the outcome of the mentalities which designed tanks or motor car bodies or Lancaster bombers. It suggests that what we want is not so much a house as a house that can be produced en masse. It is the repudiation of the individual instinct; it is the denial of variety; it is the assertion of the mind of the mass interpreted by the mass producer.

Still, it is right enough.

The public have been told that housing is a first priority after the war, and it is perhaps not surprising that those who, by the hundreds of thousands, have lived roofless in deserts and ditches—it is not surprising that they want a roof over their heads, if only to shut out the all embracing heavens.

Atkins, who is a reactionary, pours scorn upon the modern demand for housing. He says it is an artificially stimulated desire by those who have land to sell on the fringes of the cities, those who make and lay bricks, supply steel and sell slates, wallpaper, baths and water closets—this housing demand is a sales-promotion device of these interested parties. No more, he says, do we sing "Home, Sweet Home, be it ever so humble, there is no place like home." No longer do we have any pride in our hovels or think we are better off with our inconvenient, unheated, ugly houses—away with them, we say—home is not sweet—give us the Portals of Delight, or, if these fail us, let us not weary in well doing, for does not Lord Weir work for our well-being?

If a text were necessary for this conference, Atkins says, it would be "The Lord will provide. The Lord giveth, the Lord taketh away: blessed be the name of the Lord."

Lord Portal, Lord Weir—the Lord knows who!

CLUB, LONDON — Thursday

AGAIN, the sirens—hell! damnation!—and I was just going to bed to get a good night's sleep.

Damn the sirens, I said.

Down to the shelter I went. Hatch and Goldsmith were there—all these wretched widower or bachelor members of the club—I stayed for a little while and then felt I could stick it no longer, so decided to go out and risk it, whatever there was to risk.

Up Northumberland Avenue I went and crossed over the south end of Trafalgar Square. I wished I had my steel helmet and made for a doorway near Cockspur Street. It was like the good old war, I thought. It wasn't so bad then. After all, I thought, this noise, emptiness, being alone in a way, the searchlights—they were new, but it was good enough, I thought.

There were only a few Canadians over by Canada House. Good old Canadians, I thought. The barrage ceased and I moved along. There had been a soldier and a woman in the same doorway as I had been. They didn't move either. I turned back to look. They're all right, I thought. Soldier, I thought, as I passed him and his girl in the dark, you are right. Fondle her, kiss her, cling together, you are right. This is warmth, intimacy, life. Beyond, some day soon maybe, there is cold, remoteness, death. Now is all you know. This moment is yours. To-morrow—ah! to-morrow it is not yours or hers or mine, soldier. You are right, soldier. I remember, I was aloof, a crusading soldier with a purpose. I bore arms when I was a soldier. You are embraced by them. You are right, soldier, I thought, and went back to the club.

CLUB, LONDON Friday

WAR opens unseen and unexpected doors. I had not

expected to be really afraid again, but I have been. I thought I saw the last of it in the last war, but it has resurrected itself.

The experience took me back to arguments we used to have in dug-outs on the Somme—MacKinlay and Morris, Rutherford and Hall—where are they now? Hall used to argue about fear, its origin, shape, substance. His line was that fear is just a word. It can be conjured away by words. Fear is a vanity. I fear because I may find myself in some circumstance where I am not at ease, not master of myself nor master of my soul. It is a vanity and I reason I will be all right. Change means difference if you like, but one adapts onself, one learns to live anyhow, anywhere. Consider man—he proceeded in his big way—once, what is man, was chemical substances: then vegetable substances: then civilized man: then a thing like me to look back and forward: a fearful journey I have made, full of discovery. The principal discovery, however, is that you are the panic and danger, you are the anxiety and watchfulness, you are the terror—there was not at any time any cause for fear.

So he used to go on—and we. He was religious. He used to wax eloquent to his conclusion. I well remember.

> "Fear not, the counsel rings true. I, fear, am not come to destroy but to fulfil. Fulfilment casteth out fear."

There are Halls and Rutherfords to-day in and about the battle fronts and aerodromes and camps and specially, I imagine, in ships. The navy is the good society for the young man of to-day. What solace they find in talk, these boys and men. I hope some are keeping diaries. I hope all that wealth of wisdom is not to be wasted. I hope elderly bookish men like me are going to be able to read the Boswells of the Wardroom and the Messes.

HOTEL, KING'S CROSS Sunday

WE must welcome the alien, whether he be American or Australian, Canadian or Czech, New Zealander or South African, the man from Waterford or the man from Warsaw!

My alien whom I welcomed to-day is the man from Waterford, the man who would not stay at home, the Irishman who naturally looks for trouble—and finds it comes easily to his hand.

I missed my connexion by over an hour. "The 10.5 has gone, I know I have missed it." "You have, sir, indeed." "What about the next train?" I inquire. "Ah! You've missed that too," he said. "You missed it by half an hour."

What does NEXT mean? Is it "nearest" in point of time, or the following sequence in a list or record? I stand, amazed, amid the cluttered barrows and trucks. The W.A.A.F.S. and the A.T.S., the airborne and the foot soldiers surge past and around me, I look up at the sky through the broken roof. I think of a bed booked for me, unclaimed. I think of the committee assembling hours from now and I not there. I think of the war—I think of the last war—and the Boer War—and the war with the Irish in which the man from Waterford, doubtless, by his appearance took a bloody part. . . . I think and think and am lost—lost in a veritable train of thought. Thank God! That is a connexion which I can always catch! Why cannot the railway companies run their trains as I run my train of thought?

Trains! No poet has written about trains and yet what poetry lies in them—poetry when one gets them—poetry when one misses them.

EDINBURGH, HOTEL Monday

I BOUGHT Arthur Machen's "Life and Memoirs of Casanova" in the bookshop opposite the hotel—an odd place to buy a book I have always wanted, for they rarely have books of this sort.

It is the two-volume edition that my brother was so fond of—I wonder what happened to it?—men shouldn't leave their libraries to their wives—one never knows what will become of them.

If I survive this war, and my only risk is to be killed in a railway accident between King's Cross and Waverley, I intend to catalogue my books and arrange so many to be given to friends and the rest to be pulped. I don't intend the foreign eye to read my underlinings and my marginal notes. My book-plate, too, it is rather pompous and ridiculous. I don't use it now. I wouldn't use it at all if Nicolls hadn't given it me for a present.

My heart goes out to Giacomo Casanova to-night. Neither he nor I will have adventures again; none for him, and few for me. No more will he scramble over the leads after a lady love.

These pink curtains that line the heavy black-out ones—this preposterous wicker table with its pink glass top . . . this chair . . . the formal, uninviting bed—the wardrobe with carved panels—the notices on the dressing table about valuables, lighting, saving water, difficulties of service—I am in the mood of Casanova when he wrote:

> "If these Memoirs, only written to console me in the dreadful weariness which is slowly killing me in Bohemia—if these Memoirs are ever read—they will only be read when I am gone and all censure will be lost on me."

He felt safe in his writing. He remarks men are of two kinds—the ignorant and superficial, and the learned and reflective.

The latter are his public he hopes and their judgment will be in favour of veracity.

> "Why should I not be veracious? A man can have no object in deceiving himself and it is for myself that I chiefly write."

Diary-keeping scribblers like me are ever on the look out for a justification for their secret delight. We don't tell the world we are keeping a diary. It may be if we did, the world wouldn't care. There is that to it, of course, but I do it for obscurer reasons. I can think of many.

This day has been for me something. I want, if nothing else, to write its epitaph.

And again, one day, I will turn these pages and I will be dull when I am old.

But there must be better reasons.

They may be disclosed to-night in dreams.

EDINBURGH — Tuesday

I REMEMBER 1941 quite clearly. For some 1939 to 1941 are now just a blur. Events have overwhelmed memory for detail, but to-night I recall these days in London. I remember four o'clock.

Yes, I must be going, I told them in the office, it takes over two hours to get home . . . the trains . . . the buses.

And four o'clock used to be tea time in that office—clatter of cups, boiling water, one for each of us and one for the pot, yes I take two, or, no sugar for me, please, or give me a slice of lemon . . . these were good times. But at four o'clock now I must be leaving. . . . I am on duty at the post at six. . . . Mrs. M'Ardey—where is she now?—must be relieved promptly . . . her old mother, you know.

And four o'clock is it in Holland or Denmark or occupied—pre-occupied France . . . they are overhauling the bombers. Screw it up, Fritz—these wires, Hans—she's all right . . . four o'clock they're getting ready. All right. Four o'clock for all of us. . . . Tea Time deferred . . . anyway I don't care. It is not too bad. It's what I wanted. Crowded hours of glorious life . . . not quite the setting, but the stage is all right. It will do. That tea at four o'clock business was often a nuisance. They never made it quite right, it was often too strong or the water not properly boiled. In a way I am glad four o'clock means something more now than tea in the office. It will do for me, this year, next year, and if it never comes again, well, I won't grieve eternally in the place where I am going.

So I used to ruminate. I didn't think I'd survive the blitz. I had fixed it up in my mind "To cease upon the midnight"—but would there be no pain, I used to wonder.

Up here in Scotland I have felt easier. We haven't had anything really.

Clydebank was very bad and Aberdeenshire may have had troubles, but Edinburgh has been lucky. I am told it runs to a few scores but who knows? I have no curiosity. Life after 50 is really looking for the railway station from which there are no return tickets issued.

It is just as well. One way traffic is one of the ideas of the Ministry of Transport boys. They think it new!

Life has always been a one way street.

EDINBURGH Wednesday

HE shrugged his shoulders and jerked his arms. He faced me just as I was going into St. Andrew's House and said, "John Anderson, my Jo, John, when we were first acquent." I said to him, "What on earth do you mean? What gibberish is this, what incantation are you pronouncing?" "Don't you know?" he said to me, "John Anderson is in Edinburgh to-day. The Home Secretary, Minister of Home Security, Chancellor of the Exchequer and heaven knows what waits for him in the womb of to-morrow." I confessed I did not know, nor did I understand the point of his incantation.

He had been at school with John Anderson, who was educated in George Watson's College of this city, and later was a student at its University. They had been school fellows together. He knew all about John Anderson. He was an admirer of his. His own humble, unnoticed life in the Civil Service took him in other directions, but the more removed he was from his schoolfellow the more intense became his admiration.

I didn't tell him I knew Sir John Anderson probably as well as he did. My mind goes back to the days before the war when I had a good deal to do with him. I must look up my diary when next I am at home and see what my reflections were. He was something of a mystery man these days—back to the homeland with Bengal behind him and quite a reputation for great administrative ability, supported by dour—and that is a Scotch word—determination and unshakable courage. He was a great help to worried Statesmen in those days and when the time comes to tell the whole story, if it ever comes, John Anderson's place in the plan will be shown to be not less than any who looked with unshaken eyes across the menacing world, faced realistically its grimness, set about preparation for a task for which there were no precedents and no guides and no support but what a man could find in his own stout heart.

LONDON OFFICE Saturday

"DON'T be deceived by Americans" is a piece of advice I would have in railway carriages and other places where we English must be free to speak—or die. These notices about careless talk do not go far enough. We are too careless with our Americans. There is a difficulty there—and it will grow. When I speak, as I often do, to a Pole or a Frenchman or a Russian, I am aware that they are foreigners. I act accordingly. But with the Americans, because they speak the same words, they seem deceptively to need no understanding. They are quite different—in fact when I speak to an American I may be speaking to a Pole or a Frenchman or a Russian or a German or a Czech—one generation removed.

This English speech is, alas, a snare, a deception, a delusion. It makes us feel one—we think we understand—but how little that little less, and how far away that universal brotherhood to which speech is only the gateway. My hopes once were in Esperanto—or Volapuk—or a Basic

English. Alas, they faint and fail! Speech is a device to clothe and conceal thought, some diarist has declared.

Alas! I agree language may lead us towards comprehension but not to understanding. I do not despair. When we drew near to King's Cross my American drew me into the corridor and flattered me. "You are a man of the world," he said, "and I want a good time. What about it? Have you any addresses?" I was shocked. What my Minister would have replied to such an unparliamentary question I do not know. I certainly could not help him. I had no addresses except the W.V.S. or Citizens Advice Bureaux. Somehow I didn't think they would help much on this occasion.

LONDON OFFICE Monday

In the train two invaders, from the Ministry of Supply, came into my berth and sat down. "We are over an hour late" was their excuse and, of course, we must have—for are we not Civil Servants?—in this hour of uncovenanted freedom, we must have our careless talk!

Alexander was the theme; not the Alexander who was called the Great or yet Alexander who was the Grenadier, the victorious Alexander of El Alamein, but Alexander the First Lord.

The First Lord of the Admiralty has an unique place. He is Britannia: he rules the waves: he is tradition: he needs no bulwark: his home is in the deeps of Admiralty House. He, it was agreed, is an ideal Minister. He is not a sailor—though a Somerset man. He is not a politician in the rousing, rabid sense. He is true blue, none the less, true blue in the naval sense but true blue too, to his flag.

His flag—in peace and war—in industry and politics—in domestic and public life—his flag is co-operation. He really co-operates. He co-operates with the Conservatives, he co-operates with the Liberals, he co-operates with Labour. He co-operates with his colleagues.

The navy is fortunate. The Prime Minister, critics say, is part of all he has been—and how many things has he been! Chancellor of the Exchequer, Home Affairs, War and Air, Dominions, Munitions, Admiralty—none hold these offices without knowing he too has held them. He knows, does the Prime Minister, and happy these Ministers who remember it. Alexander will do well by his country. In the days that are to come, we agree, he will be a serviceable leader. He—and Woolton—they have experience and humanity and judgment. They know their fellow countrymen. They know the lights of England. They are their lights. They will sail true to them.

Like us, they will arrive at their due destination.

BEFORE BREAKFAST, HOTEL, EDINBURGH — Tuesday

IN the dim light of the bookstall at King's Cross I flutter like an ineffectual moth. I want—I know not what—I just flutter.

Penguins—they have a fishy smell—the pile of "The British Infantryman," by Ian Hay, in yellow cover, lures me not (was not I one of the First Hundred Thousand—a better but now forgotten book).

"Ah!" I sigh, *The Countryman*. I haven't seen it on the bookstalls for years and yet how refreshing is the sight of its green cover—its modest, honest, rustic face.

I buy it and am gone to my cabin. Rumbling on during the night I returned to it—to read it and to give thanks to Robertson Scott who founded it and who edits it at Idbury near Kingham in Oxfordshire. There have been more than a score of volumes of it and I think it has done more for the country than any other thing or person not excluding the many Ministers of Agriculture.

It created country life for townsmen: it confirms countrymen in their choice and it appeals to all the wisdom of the ages to justify its aims. No journal dares to set forth so consistently and so wisely its philosophy. It quotes eight lines in every issue from Virgil, Xenophon, Cicero, Cato, Washington, Job, Ecclesiastes—twice—and Paul in his own name and again in his words to the Corinthians.

It is an ever-green temptation for me, this magazine. Who at sixty, with a misspent life behind him, can resist these quoted words from Cicero?

"There is nothing better than farming, nothing more fruitful, nothing more delightful, nothing more worthy of a free man."

Punctually I arrive at the Waverley Station. With fortitude I get the lift from the station to the hotel that rises above it. With resignation I go to the room for breakfast, but it is with resolution I will go later to-day to attend the Allotments Committee at St. Andrew's House. There I will meet these twin coaxers of cabbages—these leaders of lettuces—Messrs. Scarlett & Lowe—the greatest of the market gardeners—and nothing will shake me in my regard.

They do not know the springs of my devotion. I do not tell them that I bought the latest issue of *The Countryman* for 2s. 6d. at King's Cross bookstall.

LODGINGS, EDINBURGH Wednesday

THERE was a great man lived in Edinburgh, and with a clear head and no cold I want to give him and his disciple my thanks and gratitude before I begin the day.

These steam-heated sleepers give me colds every time I travel in them these days, but I have found the sovereign cure and I will now call it always "Saintsbury."

Saintsbury was a Professor, but little of his greatness reached the common man. I found here in this bare, inhospitable place a friend who cherishes his memory and keeps it green—or is the word "golden"? My cold—it was a rheumy runner, a sniffer and a sneezer, a brain-blocker and a nose-stopper—it was all of these and had come to remain with me, so it seemed, until death do us part. But I found a friend who told me of Saintsbury. Saintsbury wrote, among much that has been forgotten apparently, an immortal work called, most modestly, "Notes on a Cellar Book."

I never saw it, but he tells in it how to make toddy, and my friend is his disciple and I am his patient. Toddy is whisky and sugar and—if you can get it—lemon. It is the method of making, the art of concoction which is of first importance. The hot bath first—and no nonsense about five inches of water either in the bath—fill it as full as you can and let it be hot. Then into bed—hot bottle—warmest pyjamas—pullover on top—socks on the feet—and, if you have one big enough, one on the head for a night-cap. Your friend is beside you. He has the ingredients. All is ready for Saintsbury.

It is according to the Morayshire rules you are told. (You needn't know what it means.) You get a bowl. First put in the hot water—sweeten it to taste—let the sugar be thoroughly melted. It is then you add the whisky—the best whisky. You do not scoff the beverage then—you ladle it nicely into a wine glass and consume as many wine glasses as you desire. Then comes a moment—you relax—you slip down below the blankets—you wave your friend away and the Sovereign Saintsbury has ascended to his throne. He summons slumber. He dethrones coughs and snorts and sneezes . . . and when the day returns all the cares that were yesterday's are gone. I render homage to Saintsbury and whisky. The Scotch are only modest in one thing: it is the virtues of whisky. Why they are so modest I cannot say. It is held by some to be the work of teetotalers who seek to make Heaven desirable by making earth intolerable and, of course, they see in this excellent beverage an obstacle insuperable.

Whisky should be the foundation of Scottish national pride. It goes all over the world with a message of goodwill. It is too dear now to be wasted on mere debauchery. It deserves a better fate. The English ought to come to the help of the Scots in this matter. They should not allow them to be so generous in allowing their best national industry to carry the major share of taxation. I implore my countrymen. Let Scotland be free from a burden we would not lay on Lancashire Cotton or Birmingham Metalware.

Let Saintsbury's Sovereign Remedy be available to all at the lowest possible price.

I have written all this before, but it is worthy of repetition.

One sings the Te Deum more than once, I hope.

IN THE TRAIN, WAVERLEY TO KING'S CROSS Friday

FOUR o'clock in the morning and I awoke in the convenient coffin which is called a sleeper.

If the dawn only occurred once every thousand years what an ado we would make of it! The poets would write poems of promise—beforehand—and blank verses of blank astonishment when they saw the spectacle itself. The newspapers would print reams about it—dawn at Constantinople, dawn at Daventry, dawn in a slum, dawn in a palace, dawn in a ditch, dawn on a dromedary, dawn everywhere—for everyone.

But it happens every morning and no one minds at all . . . except here on this train, the attendant thinks my presence in the alley way beside the compartment a little premature—if not actually unseemly. And yet it is the best of the day, I think this morning.

"Here hath been dawning another new day
Say wilt thou let it slip useless away."

If only I were afoot in these lanes and pastures this morning; these green places which slip so smoothly by me as the train races along to its destination. At eleven will I feel like this? I would like to think so. These Ministry of Supply people—they call for all the wits I have.

I remember other dawns.

Dawn on the morning of 21st March, 1918, on the left of the Fifth Army when the last German offensive of that war broke upon us. It was the last dawn for thousands. I wonder if the Prime Minister ever recollects it now—for he was there at Nurlu that very morning.

And that dawn on that Monday morning when all the City of London seemed to be on fire and only Saint Paul's

Cathedral with its golden cross still seemingly standing against the western sky.

Who the little man was I will never know, but on London Bridge he wept and I could have wept in sympathy with him. He must have been sixty and, except for the war—he told me—boy and man he had worked all his life in the city. "Over there," he said, "my life's work —my warehouse and stock and all gone up in flames." He had been brought up on a police call from Norwood to see a tragedy he could do nothing to avert.

There have been dawns and sunsets—on moors and wintry hills, a poet writes, coming in solemn beauty, but this dawn came for him in solemn tragedy.

It is three hours yet before I arrive. I get down my satchel, finger the absurd, heavy locks, open out the files. It will be tiresome, very tiresome, with the Ministry of Supply "boys," but I may as well prepare myself.

What is a dawn for these days—beauty, I imagine? Nay, says my Puritan conscience, DUTY.

HOME Saturday

HOLIDAYS at Home is the order of the day, and everywhere they are trying it, by "they" I mean the Town Councillors and other practical democrats. Priestley has had something to say about it over the air and we are all encouraging ourselves to think we like it.

The best holiday at home is one in bed. Bed is not the throne it ought to be in our horizons. We go to bed when we are tired or ill. To enjoy bed, you should go to it when you are neither tired nor ill.

Go to bed in the ordinary way, but decide the night

before "I won't get up in the morning for its nicer to lie in bed."

Seven is my usual hour but in my holiday at home period, seven is a mystic number unconnected with the 8.10 a.m. train to Waterloo. Eight is just a figure of eight. Nine is three times three—and I will have some coffee in a dressing gown. I will not catalogue further. . . . I am going to bed looking forward to a day in bed to-morrow, my holiday at home.

My table is furnished, in the presence of my foes, who are MISGIVING, DUTY, ITCH-TO-DO-SOMETHING and others omitted by John Bunyan in "Pilgrim's Progress," but, nevertheless, foes of mankind who desires truly the authentic holiday at home. The furnishments include digestive tablets, cigars and cigarettes, a siphon, a bottle, matches, a small radio set within easy reach, several books including in view of the sacredness of the occasion, "The Bible to be read as Literature."

So fortified by the rites of the Church and the Fortunate State to which I am called, I retire for a Holiday at Home.

LODGINGS, EDINBURGH Monday

TOBIAS SMOLLETT, I have only just learned, was a Scotchman. One of the eager planners showed me what he wrote about London in "Humphrey Clinker" over 150 years ago. He had the book with all his files at to-day's meeting.

Smollett then declared that London was rapidly spreading and what was open field when he last saw it was on his return covered with houses and churches. Pimlico, said the book, with Knightsbridge is joined to Chelsea and

Kensington, and the Doctor felt that in a few years all Middlesex would be covered over with bricks.

Well! Well!! and so it has come to pass and more.

In my salad days—how green was my salad!—at the end of the nineteenth century, London, though large, was tolerably so. Now it is so large as to be intolerable.

If the planners want a job they should just stop London—not another foot of field or hill—not a new building unless to replace an old—anywhere. And here in Scotland I would say the same to Glasgow, to Edinburgh too. It is time to save Edinburgh. Rebuild the city walls in the form of an immovable green belt. Thus far, and no further might be the city's motto. "Meddle wha daur" might be the wording of the notice boards all around. If a new industry comes to the city let it displace a derelict one. If it can find no derelict one, let it go to Linlithgow or Dalkeith, but let green fields lie between. I will put it forward as my plan—limitation of cities—fill up the burghs—conserve—inviolate—the countryside. It is an idea—alas! I have so few. I will tell my chairman.

EDINBURGH, ST. ANDREW'S HOUSE Tuesday

THE rises and falls of this war are significant. They are on a pinnacle and then they are engulfed, these great men. What a catalogue it is, beginning with Neville Chamberlain and the last name is not yet written.

The Ministry of Information was at the beginning a mystery . . . one almost forgets how many there were in that Ministry. There was Lord Macmillan, that exiled Scotsman who emerged from the retiring dignity of the law to the glare of the headlines, and Lord Reith followed him from the British Broadcasting Corporation. But there have been others in other fields. Where are they now?

This inevitable fortune which rules all the lives of men, distinguished and undistinguished, has been a frequent reflection of mine.

Nothing is more majestic in English Literature than that poem of Shelley's . . . "My name is Ozymandias. . . ."

"I met a traveller from an antique land. . . ." Travellers from an antique land may come and ruminate over not the ruins of London from Westminster Bridge, but the scattered ruins of our war-made reputations and war-made rejections and failures.

I have five minutes: the meeting waits but I must write the words which appeared on the pedestal of the monument in the antique land—

> "My name is Ozymandias, King of kings:
> Look on my works, ye Mighty, and despair!"

EDINBURGH — Wednesday

LET us praise famous men. Let me follow the example of Saint Matthew, who details in the first chapter of his Gospel all the begettings, except that in my case it is merely a record of all the distinguished names—a record of the important people whom I have seen in this capital of Scotland during my enforced but none the less agreeable residence.

The first and foremost, of course, is the Prime Minister, accompanied by Mr. Winant, the American Ambassador, and, in his train that day I recall Sir Stafford Cripps. That, I suppose, was the high day and holiday of this city, and there has been nothing like it since. Their Majesties, the King and Queen, when they come among us, follow a hard and literally fast programme—hard going and fast in that they move quickly to cover a very considerable field—hospitals and factories and schools, they fill the unforgiving minute and spare not themselves.

I will recall, too, when I peruse this book in days to come, the Duke of Kent and his Duchess, the Duke of Gloucester and his Duchess . . . all the Royal Family have been to Scotland during my stay. I think all the Politicians too—I come back to them in the catalogue—the Scottish politicians—Mr. Johnston, Mr. Westwood, Mr. Woodburn, now fill the bill that formerly was filled by Mr. Colville, Mr. Brown, Captain M'Ewen and Mr. Scrymgeour-Wedderburn . . . all these figures have gone and some of them have gone on, but all of them enriched the Scottish scene.

Great events have taken place in the Usher Hall, and some I was privileged to attend—others I sought to attend and was unable to get admission or was preoccupied with what doubtless was thought to be more important public affairs.

The Usher Hall of this city has seen the Prime Minister get his Freedom, the Chancellor of the Exchequer, the Secretary of State, the Prime Minister of New Zealand, and it has also seen great speeches by the Foreign Secretary (Mr. Eden made a great impression), and Sir Archibald Sinclair in the Salute to Russia Week, when his eloquence evoked admiration and praise from the younger generation who had not known the heights to which Liberal oratory could rise; and, in the same place, Sir Kingsley Wood and Lord Woolton held a vast concourse spellbound.

And so I write them all down, somewhat idly, this evening, because I know I am coming near to the end of my days in this capital. Soon they will be a memory, a recollection, and I want to be able to go to this book and turn the pages and so recapture something that seems lost. I wonder if I am not being converted to the alternative view of time, to the possibility that things stand for ever and that we pass on, that there is no such thing as time but we are only flying observers of it and that these events are ever there; I have merely passed by the side of them.

Priestley had a play—what was that play, "Time and the Conways"? was that the play?—I have forgotten. I went to see it with Bonar Thompson. Bonar Thompson has left Hyde Park now. What a considerable influence he had over the crowds. When I get home I must look at his book again, if I have not lost it. Its title was "The Hyde Park Orator."

LONDON — Friday

It rather shocks me.

When his boy was killed over France, I knew that Jenkins felt it more than he showed. He went about his business, of course, but there was too much of the stoic in him. His restrained grief, his consistent, unabated, patient application to his duty did not deceive me; it camouflaged—for there is no better description—a broken heart. Being in the last war himself, and seeing so many of the lovely lads who were his friends go to death and rottenness, made him feel that his own boy was doubly dear. Pride merged with clutching, gnawing apprehension when his boy got his medal at Buckingham Palace and so eagerly went back to it again, and now it has happened.

The story is told; the chapters are all finished.

His wife, fortunately, in a way, went before him and, like Edmund Burke, he felt he lived in an unfriendly world, that those who should have stayed to see him go had left him, alone and lamenting. They called it heart failure, but does the heart fail when it breaks?

I wonder if I am right to go on as I do. This is a tiring, wearing life and I have no wish to be a casualty this war, the battle stations of which are Waverley and King's Cross.

I want a time out of the line. I want to withdraw for a little and prepare my soul to meet my God.

OFFICE, EDINBURGH Tuesday

"PASSED to you, please," is a cutting from Hansard in which the Chancellor of the Exchequer indicates the advertising costs of the various departments. This is an entirely new departure and, as a Government servant, I don't like to think that two million pounds nearly, was spent on advertising the various activities of the administration. Old fashioned Civil Servants—if there are any remain—must wag their heads gravely at this departure. The Ministry of Food seems to spend most but I notice that the National Savings Movement in Scotland and England had over half a million between them. This might be considered an appropriate douceur for the press, but there may be other views. In any case, the press give most liberal publicity and, from what I know of them, they are as generous and public-spirited as any other section of the public.

These reflections are "not up my street" as they say, although our own department also spends money in this way. It is the Savings Movement that I challenge and I challenge it because I have still warm recollections of a tour which I made here in Edinburgh with the redoubtable Mr. Wells, Secretary of the Scottish Savings Committee under the leadership of Lord Alness.

As we went round one place and another and met the women collectors of the Savings Movement in church halls, in private houses and later at a rally in the City Chambers, what I gathered was that this, of all the movements which the war has brought into being, was the most economical. These devoted women—for the collectors mostly are women—pad the hoof from door to door, with no special allowance for shoe leather, no uniforms, no flags or banners waving . . . only a small, metal badge by way of authority. It struck me as being such an economical movement that I must say this extract from Hansard leaves me a little shaken. When the committee come forward so generously and voluntarily and give their strength, their leisure, their time, is it necessary to impose a heavy expense of this character upon a movement which prides itself in being voluntary? This amount of advertising given to the Savings Banks would have seemed a fortune and even to the big banks would have seemed an enormous sum of money for stimulating savings by advertising. I think those who know the business should do it and if they are permitted to have voluntary workers they should be allowed the honour and glory of being voluntary, unpaid workers and not have their banner sullied by the insignia of paid and unnecessary advertising.

I am going out to-night to Gorgie (I never know whether the second "G" is soft or hard, I believe it is hard) and there I will see the Gorgie women's depot with Mrs. Eltringham Miller and hear what she has to say. I have never found her lacking in effective speech.

HOTEL, EDINBURGH — Wednesday

After one of many visits to the bookshops of this delectable city, I look at my purchases piled on the table in this now familiar but never fondly loved bedroom.

The Scotch show up well among the publishers. John Murray—a good Scotch name—whose present head, Sir John Murray, led the Royal Scots in 1918; and there's Macmillan—whose Harold Macmillan, M.P., I remember away back in 1935 joined with Joad and L. P. Jacks, with H. G. Wells and St. John Ervine and many others in producing a manifesto and a programme called "The Next Five Years" (I wonder if that book is still in print?). Constables, Chambers, Collins, Blackie, Nelsons, Blackwood—they all have the brand of the thistle on them in varying degree. Edinburgh has its resident publishers, too. Very much a Scotsman, I have remarked Hodge, the publisher of law and crime books. He has been compelled to admit my acquaintance—a lover of music rather than civil servants. On occasions I have forced myself upon him—this member of the Crimes Club. He, like me, travels from Waverley to King's Cross. I reflect he is the only publisher I know. He has an English name; likes beer which he drinks because the doctor told him to—how many years ago? It was in Leipzig—he had a cold. The wise doctor prescribed two pints as a minimum in the evening before retiring and the wise Hodge has never neglected the prescription and preserved his health accordingly.

Presto! I will see him and beg him to publish the less libellous parts of my diary.

It is an idea. I will accost him on his way up the Mound to his publishing office. It is a stiffish climb—he walks up the west side—and he will not be able to refuse consideration of the idea. I fancy he likes me—but I dismiss the thought. Apart from music and his doctor's prescription he appears to prefer criminals to civil servants.

HOTEL, EDINBURGH Thursday

THIS always has been a place of religion. Here is holy ground—the Scots have been saying for centuries.

It began, it is true, with the Castle.

Stow's Chronicles place its beginnings as far back as nine hundred and eighty-nine years before Christ, when Ebranke (who had "twenty-one wyves of whom he receyved twenty sonnes and thirty daughters) made the castell of Maydens, now called Edenbrough."

Two thousand years later there came the Abbey of Holyrood and since then Edinburgh has never been far away from the Kirk.

Its religious practices are everywhere apparent. It has more churches than any city I have seen or heard of and even its secular establishments are conducted under the patronage of the Saints. Saint Cuthbert's Co-operative Society supplying thousands of citizens with beef and boots, funerals and furniture, is the most notable example, and there is even a football team known by the name of Saint Bernard's.

The Scotch Clergy are to be seen at football matches. To-day I have seen a former Moderator of the Church of Scotland at one, and none the worse for it; a Moderator being an annually elected Archbishop, if one is to find a doubtful English parallel. They are great preachers, these Ministers—eloquent men who for half an hour can expound and expand, illustrate and embellish half a dozen words of a text from the Bible.

Their General Assembly is their annual meeting, to which the King must come or send a worthy representative and declare his loyal adherence to the Kirk and all its doctrines. I was amazed at the discovery—I simply couldn't believe it—but it has gone on since the days when the Scotch gave us their Kings to rule over both England and Scotland.

It gives me great pleasure to explain all this to my colleagues who know less than I do. They are facetious about the Union of England and Scotland and I have to discourage the unseemly jest that the Union of the Crowns was due to Scottish economy—an agreed device to pass on the major cost of government to the English.

Someone sent me anonymously, in an O.H.M.S. envelope, a book called "The Unspeakable Scot," but it has left me unshaken.

I like the Scotch and their grave, dignified ministers of religion, as I have seen them passing in droves up the Mound about their Father's business.

EDINBURGH Friday

THIS planning—is there not too much of it? I have a memorandum to write but I calm myself with these pages of my diary first.

Pepys did that, his diary was his father confessor—it heard all, knew all, and very easily, forgave all. It saw Samuel Pepys as a reasonable creature, justified in all he did by good—or, anyway—irresistible reasons.

My gorge rises against planners. Who are they? Smith

of the Ministry of Works, Jones of the Ministry of Health, Robinson of the Ministry of Labour—who are they to take the liberties from the fighting men—who are they to order their future behind their backs while they are taking their orders from their Commanders in the battle?

Planning is a denial of liberty. Battling in Italy—bombers over Berlin—leagues under the sea in a submarine—men plan a small garage, a milk round, a job as an advertising man and Messrs. Smith, Jones, and Robinson decide that there are to be no more ugly roadside garages, that milk will be municipalized or co-operated, and that advertising is wasteful and interferes with ordered production. They plan, but their planning takes away liberty of choice for thousands of better men.

This won't do.

I can't put this in my memorandum.

I will need to think again.

LONDON Saturday

THEY rise very quickly but they disappear almost as quickly from public life. It is not many months ago since the name of General Dobbie, the hero of Malta, was in everyone's mind. It is an epic story how, in what was by no means a united community, this stout, distinguished soldier held the Island of Malta against all the forces of the evil one. It is a story which they have told us on the radio and one has read about it in the papers, but I have had it from the lips of sailormen of all sorts who have been there and took action.

Looking at Malta on the map, one wonders how we held it in '39, in '40, and '41, but, looking at Dobbie as I saw him, one feels one has the clue. General Dobbie is, I think, fortunately for his country, not a man who allows much debate or argument within himself. His duty is presented to him, he is assigned to his place, he takes up his stand and he has no argument with destiny—"here I am set, here I stand and that Hand that places me here will be the Hand that removes me." Dobbie is the embodiment of doggedness and determination. A more intellectual man, I opine, might have had some doubts.

Organizing adequate defence, the uncertain attitude of the people of the island, the religious and racial differences . . . all these, to men of good judgment and open minds, might well have brought about another decision than that which Dobbie took. Dobbie, fortunately, had nothing of Hamlet in him; he found himself inspired by a positivism which is as old as the ruins of Palestine. In the last resort it is the Dobbies who save cities and countries, the unbeatable ones, the undefeatable, those who cannot see anything but victory, those who, like the Prime Minister in May, 1940, saw clearly that their portion is blood, toil, tears, and stood and accepted it. . . . Men like the Prime Minister who have stood from the beginning with only one aim, with only one purpose to which they give their lives, and that is victory, at all costs victory, and in spite of all difficulties victory, however hard and long the road may be.

Let us give thanks to the Dobbies and hope that under God's mercy the supply will never fail, undeserving though we may be of such blessings.

LONDON Wednesday

HE has been very kind. Both the Permanent Secretary and the Minister have been very kind. I felt like a schoolboy standing rather at attention while the Minister spoke his piece.

"Yes, I will sit down."

Seated in the leather chair, the Minister, elbows on his desk, changed his fountain pen from right to left. I heard how admirably I had done—loyalty—unwearied devotion to the department—no trouble spared—sympathetic understanding with colleagues—with other departments—admirable contacts with local authorities and the general public—model of what a distinguished Civil Servant should be.

I heard it all and through it all there was the grinding of the wheels that have carried me so often from King's Cross to Waverley. The Minister's words seemed somehow to join up with the rhythmic regularity of sound, as sad, as unrelenting as destiny itself. His voice tailed off. In his best public speeches he is emphatic, dynamic, at the beginning but tails off into an insinuating, rather quiet appeal. I have often thought that he would be better to begin with the quiet appeal and end with the dynamic assertion, but that has not been his way, either then or in what I now know is my last interview.

"You will be hearing from me." I understand that apparently my name will go forward for consideration by His Majesty the King. "For Public Services," I take it, will be the label. But I have a sense of relief. I will not wait until the war is over. There are others, eager, hungry, who want to make the journey from King's Cross to Waverley and Waverley to King's Cross. I will go back to my home and I will eat, drink, and sleep, rejoin the wardens and take my share of night duty, and if there is anything more coming to us from the Germans, I will do what I can to offer it an appropriate welcome.

HOME Thursday

HISTORY doesn't tell what the owner of the colt thought when it was taken for the ride to Jerusalem and history is equally mute on what the money changers said when their stalls were cast out of the temple. History is like most women. It tells us a lot we don't want to know and is silent on things about which one's curiosity is alert and questioning.

This book tells some of the things an ordinary citizen thought and did in these years of 1939 to 1944.

If these years included the finest hour of his country these pieces of writing then are a footnote to history and so worth writing. I am all for the footnotes—the P.B.I. of literature. The top notes are for the top-notchers, the footnotes for the footmen.

Some day you and I will be the subject matter of the historians; what we did and thought and wrote will be interesting to a generation which will think itself, but be mistaken, incidentally, better than its ancestors.

It is dull for me to rake over the ashes of the past—my own especially—but it is something to poke fun at posterity. They are an unhumorous lot, the unborn.

"Visions of glory, spare my aching sight, Ye unborn ages, crowd not on my soul!" Is it Wordsworth? I can't find it.

POSTSCRIPT, VIDE PRESS

"MR. TIMOLEON has resigned his post in the Ministry and has been thanked by the Minister for his services. He was awarded a C.B.E. in the Birthday Honours this year."

INDEX OF NAMES